The Asquinn Twins
Book Four
Sihon

Grace Brooks

PUBLISHED by PARABLES
Earthly Stories with a Heavenly Meaning

The Asquinn Twins Book 4: Sihon

Original Copyright©2008 / 2015 Heather Radford / Grace Brooks
Orginally The Asquinn Twins Series
 Written as The Asquinn Twins and Grant
Revised 2015 © Heather Radford / The Asquinn Twins: Sihon

All right to the contents of this book are reserved for the author

Published By Parables
June, 2018

All Rights Reserved. No part of this book may be reproduced or utilized in any form or by any means, electronic or mechanical, including photocopying, recording, or by any information storage and retrieval system, without permission in writing from the author.

Unless otherwise specified Scripture quotations are taken from the authorized version of the King James Bible.

ISBN 978-1-945698-60-6

Printed in the United States of America

Readers should be aware that Internet Web sites offered as citations and/or sources for further information may have been changed or disappeared between the time this was written and when it is read.

The Asquinn Twins
Book Four

Sihon

Grace Brooks

Published by Parables
Earthly Stories with a Heavenly Meaning

Acknowledgment

Special thanks goes out to my mentor who helped me through this book, Lauren Carter. Lauren Carter is also from Ontario but now resides in The Pas, Manitoba. She is a professional author, taught writing at university and served as Writer in Residence in The Pas, Manitoba, Canada.

A Word From The Author

    This is a work of fiction, which means all the characters are conjured up through the imagination and there are no real life counterparts. Anyone who knows the James Bay Frontier or Timiskaming District areas in the northern portion of the province of Ontario, Canada will recognize the setting for this story and the series. Although I have used the right names for most of the towns, cities and rivers, I used a fictitious name for the town at my discretion.

    The characters are all figments of my imagination.

        The idea for the series did spring from an incident concerning Mom and the Ontario Provincial Police, that nipped my life of crime in the bud. Instead of being bitter towards the OPP and holding a grudge for this I will forever be grateful and hold a deep respect for the Ontario Provincial Police. This has spanned the years, even though I do not live in Ontario anymore.

    It's to the Ontario Provincial Police Force I dedicate the entire series.

Chapter One
A Visitor For The Summer

Martin and Sihon walked together towards a tall, two story light green frame house.

Sihon had just returned from checking the mail and carried a single white envelope,opened, in his hand. Sihon would be thirteen. He wore grey and white, ankle high, laced up sneakers, light blue jeans and a yellow T-Shirt. His brown hair cut short.

Martin would be in his late twenties. He parted his brown hair on the left side and brushed the hair to the right. He taught grades nine to twelve at the Golden Ridge Baptist School Forest Lake. Today he wore black causal pants, black oxfords and green and black checked short sleeved shirt.

Sihon and Martin entered the house and kitchen.

"Good afternoon, Dad, Sihon," Fourteen year old Olvina Asquinn said.

Sihon made his way across the laminated kitchen floor, over to the long mahogany brown wooden table in the middle of the room. To him this house was the perfect, and the family every kid wanted to live with. The house overflowed with love and laughter.

Five girls already sat at the table. All were fourteen years old quintruplets, and resembled each other, but were not identical. Sihon pulled a chair away from the table and sat down. He rested his elbows on the oil table cloth. He set the envelope on the table in front of him.

"I've been summoned to Cameron Estate, Uncle Conrad's summer residence. I don't want to go."

He looked at the adult at the table. "Good afternoon, Audrey."

Audrey wore her shoulder length brown hair done up in a bun at the back of her head.

Then Sihon's eyes went from one of his foster sisters to the other. "Olvina, Pheobe, Kathleen, Cassia, Eunice."

Audrey jumped up from the wooden chair and rushed to Martin to welcome him home. Her long, ankle length peasants skirt swirled as she did so. "Welcome to the dinner table, dearest," she said, her brown eyes shining with love. "Did you have a good morning at school with the children writing final exams?"

"Yes, thank you," Martin answered.

"I'm relieved to have this school year over with. I have only one examim to write this afternoon" Sihon said. He turned and looked out the tall kitchen window by the sink, then the picture window in the living room. The bottom portions had been pushed up. A gentle breeze blew in through the screens. The ivory colored curtains were open, so all could see the blue sky outsides Sihon sighed, and said, "Ah, the beginning of the summer holidays."

" How nice it is to have an entire summer to ourselves," Olvina said. She was the oldest of the quintuplets; her sandy colored hair grew thick and shiny down to her waist. She kept hair out of her eyes and off her face by wearing a plastic gold coloured hair band. Her brown eyes sparkled with the joy of life. Like her sisters, she wore a denim culottes, a garment that actually was a split skirt but flexible as jeans. There were also the the version that looked like long legged pants; these also came in shorts.

She and her four sisters had been adopted by Martin and Audrey when the set were babies. Martin and Martha were unable to have children of their own.

Kathleen was the middle baby of the quintuplets. With her blackhair and brown eyes, she didn't resemble any of the rest. Her hair grew to her shoulders and curled outwards and upwards. She wore bangs down to her eyebrows.

Martin said, "Time to quit the chatter. Sihon, would you please pray?"

When all were silent with heads bowed, Sihon asked God to bless the food.

Bowls were filled with soup sitting in a shiny metal container in the middle of the table, sandwiches were taken from a plate handy.

Sihon chewed his spam and lettuce sandwich in silence. Martin glanced at him as the boy's silence lengthened.

"Something on your mind, Sihon?"

Sihon sighed loudly."Yeah. I've been summoned to Uncle Conrad's place, Cameron Estate, on Georgian Bay. I don't understand why it's Uncle Conrad and Aunt Lillian that's taking me in for the summer? Why isn't it Dad and Mom?"

"I hear your parents spend the summer at Cameron Estates, too," Martin said. He pointed at the letter beside Sihon's plate, "May I read it?'

Sihon handed him open letter.

"I've heard talk from you and Audrey and other members of the family, that Uncle Conrad and Aunt Lillian hate anything Christian," Sihon mused as Martin read. " Why do I have to go at all? Why go there?"

"Sihon, listen to me," Martin said gently. He folded the letter and handed the paper back to Sihon. "When you were brought to us by the police, Ken, and the child welfare lady, you were only two and a half years old. Your parents, aunt and uncle abused you and you needed to be placed in a caring, loving home, immediately. Audrey and I were chosen. We did not officially adopt you. We are fostering you."

"I know all that," Sihon said.

"What this all means, Sihon, is that your parents can take you back anytime they think is convenient. It sounds like the family want another chance with you. "

"But I don't want to go," Sihon said. "This is my family."

Martin emptied his bowl. His two sandwiches were also consumed in a hurry. He pushed back his chair and stood up.

"I must get back to the school. High School is out for the summer, but not grades one to eight. I promised Aunt Charlotte I'd help this afternoon. You girls are basking in the knowledge that you completed your first year of high school successfully. Sihon, you will be free to do what you want , you don't have exams to write after this afternoon."

"All I have to do is remember to show up at the school house in fourteen days to get my report card."

"I don't envy you in that hot schoolroom this afternoon, Martin dearest."Audrey stood up and kissed her husband.

Olvina sprang to her feet and rushed to her father, "Have a good afternoon of teaching, Dad."

Phoebe followed her sister. Phoebe also wore her hair to the shoulder. Her hair curled upwards and outwards. She parted her hair on the left, with no bangs.

Phoebe hugged and kissed her father. "I will think of you all afternoon in that hot schoolroom."

Phoebe stepped aside and Kathleen kissed her father on the cheek, but didn't say anything. Cassia and Eunice hugged their adoptive Dad, but like Kathleen, did not delay him further with words.

Cassia's hair had a light reddish tinge to it, and grew to her shoulders, curling upwards and outwards. She parted her hair in the middle and flipped half over one shoulder.

Eunice wore her hair straight to the shoulder, no parts, bangs to the tip of her eyes.

Martin went out the side door just as two boys the girls' age entered the entrance enclosure.

"Hi, there, Mr. Asquinn," one boy, a dark Metis youth greeted him. He had been the girls and Sihon's best friend from grade one. He wore crumpled, unwashed hand-me-down clothes. His hair hadn't been cut in awhile.

"Hi, Uncle Martin," the second, a white youth, greeted Martin. He was the girls' first cousin, approximately the same age and in the same grade in school. His clothes were not brand new, but washed, ironed, and mended. His hair washed and shiny.

" Go on in, Trev, Wapinkino."

In the kitchen, Audrey looked at her daughters, "Cassia, Eunice, Kathleen, dish clean up time. Olvina, Phoebe, do what ever you want, it's free time for you."

Chair legs scraped wood as chairs were pushed back. Cassia, Kathleen and Eunice went to the linen cupboard at the end of the kitchen cupboards. Kathleen got there first, so opened the door and handed out clean, crisp aprons to her two sisters to put on over their culottes and blouses. Eunice put the loop of her apron over her head and tied the string Eunice started clearing the table of the meals dishes. Cassia carried some dishes to the double stainless steel sinks, wet a dish cloth and wiped the table clean.

Trevor led the way to the table.

"Wapinkino," Eunice said.

"And Trevor," Olvina said.

Phoebe invited, "Please, sit down."

Wapinkino didn't sit. He moved over to the kitchen cupboards where Kathleen leaned over the sink washing dishes. He leaned against the cupboard close to her.

"Will you have a glass of milk?" Kathleen said.

Wapinkino said, "No. But thanks."

" I just ate, Trevor said. "

"We don't see enough of you lately," Olvina stated.

Everyone had a good laugh at this.

"Olvina, we only started vacation today. You saw Trev and Wapinkino lots during the school year." Cassia said. "Lorne, Earl and Owen all three have paying jobs. And Trev works along side his father with the railroad- an engineer even." She drained the sink of dirty dish water and spread powered cleanser, and scrubbed until the aluminum shone.

"I know. A working man doesn't have spare time for much of a social life. Mr. Winschell keeps Owen busy," Wapinkino said.

Wapinkino looked at Sihon. "Trev and I are going for a swim, wanna come?"

Sihon pushed back his chair and was on his feet immediately. "I can't," he said. "I have an exam to write."

Olvina and Phoebe ran outside. Their cousin and Sihon followed, but Larry stayed.

"Wapinkino doesn't want to leave Kathleen's side," Phoebe said and giggled. "Larry loves Kathleen."

"But does Kathleen love Wapinkino?" Olvina asked.

Wapinkino came out of the house. Before he and Trevor and Sihon could start towards the beach below Golden Ridge, across the railroad tracks, Trevor said, "Lets go to the public beach today."

"Good idea," Wapinkino said.

"Have fun," Sihon said. "I don't want to fail Geography for not showing up to write the exam."

The old Forest Lake one-roomed public school house had been closed. The school district officials had deemed it useless to keep the school going as very few children enrolled. Golden Ridge Baptist Church kept the school active by buying the building and using it for a Christian School. The school had been renovated into a two roomed building. In one room grades one to eight were taught. Charlotte Turehue Asquinn, the police chief superintendent's wife, walked the aisles as the children concentrated on the questions in front of them. Charlotte and Ken had a family of five boys. There was Murray the oldest at twenty-one and worked as an anchor man at a television station. Or he did. He'd quit the job and would be entering police College in the fall. He was married and his wife expecting. Kirk, eighteen and set up to enter Police College in the fall, then seventeen year old Brian, fourteen year old Raymond, and eleven year old Sydney.

In the grade eight classroom Sihon was seated, bent over sheets of papers, pens and pencils in hand, wrote his final tests. Only one other girl was in the room. A blonde girl named Vanessa Vanladisave.

Because the high school children were free of school for the summer, Martin was not in the second portion of the school. These rooms stood empty. Martin used up the rest of the school year helping his sister-in-law supervise the children writing their finals. There was a third lady in the room.

Martha Asquinn-Turehue, Martin's identical twin sister, and also Ken's sister. Martha married Staff Sergeant Bradan Turehue, the second in command with the Ontario Provincial Police detachment in Forest Lake. Bradan and Martha had a family of four. Gerald, the oldest at twenty-one, worked with his cousin, Murray, as anchor in the six o'clock news cast. Next came Lyle, who, at eighteen, was all eager to start police acadamy in the fall. And next fifteen year old Shannon and twelve year old Joanne.

Martha was a registered Public Health Nurse. She, too, agreed to spend the rest of the year helping out Charlotte.

A window stood open to allow breezes from the lake to blow through. Sound of teen-agers enjoying the hot afternoon, carried by the breeze to Sihon. He looked up, glanced out the window annoyed at the disruption.

Quietly, Martha moved over to the window and closed it.

"Thank you, Mrs. Turehue," Sihon said.

Sihon finished answering the last question. He looked at the hand clock on one wall. Three O'clock. Charlotte glanced at him and walked silently over to his seat.

"Are you finished writing your exam, Sihon?"

"Yes, Mrs. Asquinn," replied Sihon.

"Give it to me, then," Mrs. Asquinn said. Sihon's teacher took the paprers from Sihon. "Go and join your friends at the beach. I know you've longed to all afternoon."

Vanna raised her hand, indicating she's also finished writing. But Sihon didn't wait. He was out the open school doors in a flash and running towards home. He quickly changed into his bathing suit, and after redressing, was out of the house in seconds. He crossed the road in front of their home and walked along a well used path that led up to the railroad tracks. This path continued down the other side of the railroad embankment to some docks and a lesser used beach. Sihon did not go down to the docks, but turned west on the railroad. Ahead he saw Phobe and Olvina.

The tracks ran right through the village of Forest Lake between the houses themselves and the lake. In spite of the railroad track, most houses in Forest Lake enjoyed a spectacular view of Wan Asquinn and the main body of Lake Forest beyond. The bay had been named Wan Asquinn or Asquinn Bay by Martin and his brother Ken shortly after Obediah Asquinn moved his family there

The family consisted then of Ken, the oldest, Martin and his twin sister, Martha, and Eric, a baby in arms. Faith, Tim and Vincent were born later in the James Bay Frontier.

Sihon ran to catch up with the girls. A half mile from home, the three left the track and followed another well used path to the public beach and joined the boys. The boys had already grown tired of swimming and had pulled on jeans over top of wet swimming trunks, then pulled on T shirts, socks and shoes. Trevor sat down beside Olvina, on her right side where she and her sister sat where the sand met the grass. There was a natural ledge here. Wapinkino sat down beside Phoebe on her left.

A boy with hair so fair it was almost white, and the girls' age, and a companion strolled towards Sihon's group. They paused in front of Wapinkino and Phoebe.

"Hi, Lorne, Earl," Olvina and Phoebe said together. Earl was Vanna's sister.

"Are you staying with your aunt and uncle's at Van Ladisavs Marina and Boat Tours, Earl?" Wapinkino asked.

"That's right, Snow Owl" Earl said.

"It's just like you to use the English translation of the Native word, Wapinkino," Sihon said. "Snow Owl."

"I'll be there all summer, learning the business from uncle. He does expect me to take over the marina once I'm finished school."

"We know," Sihon, Wapinkino, Trevor, Olvina, and Phoebe answered in unison.

"Vanna is writing an exam right now. She wants to be home with mom and dad until school starts in the fall. Then we both will board out here again and attend the Christian school."

"I hope you board with us," Phoebe said.

"Where's Kathleen?" Lorne inquired.

"She stayed at home to help Mom out," Olvina said.

"So did Cassia and Eunice," Phoebe added.

"let's go in the water," Sihon said.

"No, thanks, I've had enough of the lake for today," Wapinkino said. Trevor was on his feet in a flash. "Yeah."

"Lets," Earl said.

"I'm game," Trevor said.

Wapinkino followed Trevor's lead and peeled off his clothes down to his swim trunks.

"Let's go," Sihon said. "Last one in is a rotten egg."

Five boys charged towards the water. Olvina and Phoebe laughed at the playful shoving. Sihon started out in the lead, and remained there. He splashed into the water, then ran out aways until the water deepened. Here he dove right in.

On shore Phoebe looked at Olvina, "Don't you wish we could join the boys?"

Olvina nodded.

When Trevor resurfaced, Wapinkino was right there to splash him.

A week later Sihon was returning home at noon, with his report card. He reread the report as he walked, smiling. A girl his age joined him on the road in front of his home, just before turning up their driveway. Her hair was light blonde, but not as light as her brother Earl's hair.

"Hi, Vanna."

"Did you pass?" Vanna asked.

"Yes. I will be in grade nine next year.

"High School, for both of us. Sihon, I'd love to have you join us for a car ride this evening."

"No. Thanks."

Vanna said loudly, "How silly of you."

Sihon said nothing.

"If you change your mind, call me," Vanna said and stomped off.

"I won't change my mind," Sihon called after her.

Sihon went inside. Standing in the porch he could hear the hum of voices in the kitchen. He listened for awhile, then his face lit up as a burst of laughter reached him. Sihon walked as silently as he could into the room and sat down .

Martin asked the blessing on the food.

Sihon retreated to his room right after supper that evening. He sat down in a chair, amidst the clutter of packed suitcases, beside the window and stared out at the tree tops bending in the wind. Seeing it was only the start of summer, at seven o'clock, the sun was still high in the sky. He could plainly see objects outside.

In the ally way running between residential property and school property, he saw Chief Superintendent and his second in command, approaching from the west. Both men would in their early forties. Neither officer wore a hat to cover his crew cut. Sihon could see clearly that the Chief Superintendent and Sergeant's sideburns were silver and silver hairs sprinkled through their head. Both men had dreamed since boyhood about joining the Ontario Provincial Police and keeping the bad guys at bay. While teens, this desire changed to being part of the Royal Canadian Mounted Police. So Ken and Bradan, along with their new brides, Charlotte and Martha, left Forest Lake. Ken and Bradan trained at the academy in Regina. Neither were happy, and concluded God wanted them in Forest Lake, protecting and serving the public there. So both men quite the RCMP, came back to Ontario and joined the Ontario Provincial Police.

As they passed by the driveway into Martin's house, Sihon called out through the screen in the window, "Hi, Mr. Asquinn. Hi, Mr. Turehue. It's nice to know the Ontario Provincial Police are out there protecting us."

The officers stopped and turned to where the voice originated.

"Thank you, Sihon," Ken said.

"Such kind words," Bradan said. The partners continued their foot patrol.

Olvina, with Cassia beside her, stood in the doorway watching him. Cassia followed as Olvina stepped further into the room, stepping around packed suitcases, and stopped beside him.

"Feeling down, Sihon?" Olvina asked

Sihon gasped, startled. "Oh, Olvina. Cassia, I didn't even realize anyone else was in the room."

"Want to talk about it?" Olvina said. "I want to talk to you one more time before you go home."

"It would be nice. Do you have the time?"

"We sure do,"   Olvina said.

Sihon moved from the chair he occupied, in order to allow Olvina a place to sit. Cassia settled in one corner of the bed next to Sihon. Once the three were comfortable, he said, "Where do I belong?"

The bluntness of the boy's question surprised Olvina. She had to think several seconds before she could answer. "Where do you think you belong?"

"Do I really belong in this Christian family? Is my place with my aunt and uncle? I don't know. Do I belong here with Martin and Audrey and you girls while my cousin Crystal is at home with her parents, my aunt and uncle? Children still learn about God here. They never go to church at home."

"Did some of the kids tease you about living here?" Cassia said.

"No," Then he blushed, having told a lie. "Maybe a little."

"Who?" Olvina said.

"Vanna, just a little," Sihon said. "I don't have the solution. I can't come up with any answers that make sense. "

Olvina put a reassuring hand on Sihon's shoulder. "Aunt Martha would say, the feelings you've expressed are normal, don't worry about anything. We love you here."

"Oh sure, then why am I being sent away? "

"You weren't breaking up your family, Sihon. You are better off here, believe me. You won't have much of an opportunity to make anything of yourself if you remain with your father,"

"But Mom and Dad, what about them? What about Crystal? It isn't clear why I can call Mr. Cameron, Uncle."

"Dad always told us this relationship between Asquinns and Camerons goes back a long way. Both families are rooted deeply in Wales. Arthur Cameron, Mr. Conrad Cameron and Mr. Nigel Weistein, your father, and Pastor Asquinn, our grandfather, are really distant cousins. You call Mr. Cameron Uncle because he's Aruthur Caneron's son, your uncle and Crystal is your first cousin. Arthur Cameron is supposed to be your grandfather."

"You aren't making any sense, Olvina," Sihon said. "It sounds to me like relationships in the families go back so far in time it's difficult to sort out uncles, aunts, and cousins. It doesn't make sense any sense. I don't understand it." Tears wet the corners of Sihon's eyes. "I don't want any part of the Camerons."

Sihon turned his head, shutting out any further discussion. He tried to be brave and hold back the tears from spilling down his cheeks, but they did in spite of his efforts. He missed the pitying glance Olvina favored him with.

"That's what's making you ill. Right?" Cassia inquired. "You're afraid of what's awaiting you at home; the rejection from your father and mother, Uncle Conrad's spite for you and all that. Am I right?"

Sihon gasped, and then mumbled, "How did you know? Yes. I like it here. I like going to the Christian school here in Forest Lake."

He stood up and lifted the curtain on the window facing north and looked out at the school sitting on top of the little knoll. Facing the main road a sign painted on a wooden sign in big black letters stood, GOLDEN RIDGE BAPTIST SCHOOL.

"I want to come back to classes in the Christian school in September.

Sihon then shifted his gaze to the west where the Baptist church stood on a ridge.

" I like hearing the story about how your Tadcu and Mamcu moved the family from Wales to start a church, and settled in this little village of Forest Lake in a south eastern portion of the James Bay Frontier. He'd been sent out by a Baptist church in Wales to start a Missionary Baptist Church. This he did and named it Golden Ridge Baptist Church.

"You will," Olvina assured the youth.

"Of course I will. I love attending church services in that building, and most of all, love hearing redemption's story. My home is with this household. Nothing can change that," Sihon said.

CHAPTER TWO
Cameron Estate

Uncle Conrad drove the rusty coloured Oldsmobile through scenic farming country along the shore of Georgian Bay. Uncle Conrad would be Ken and Beadan's age, forty-one. Silver also was scattered through Uncle Conrad's hair. He was good-looking in a dark way. His facial features seemed set in stone. When he smiled it seemed more like a snarl than a joyful greeting. Aunt Lillian was petite, her face painted with an overload of makeup, she wore a mini-skirt.

Sihon gazed out the back side window. The beauty of the area enthralled him. Aunt Lillian rode in the front on the passenger side of the middle console. Crysta, Uncle Conrad and Aunt Lillian's daughter, and Sihon's first cousin, shared the back seats.

Conrad turned off the wide highway onto a smaller road. Wide green pastures and well maintained fences stretched away from the road as far as the eye could see. Black and white cattle grazed in the fields, further along fine looking horses grazed. Even further along Sihon saw potatoes, corn, carrots, cabbages, lettuce, and radishes growing in great abundance in fine, rich soil.

"Is this your property, Uncle Conrad?"

The woman beside his uncle in the front seat looked back at him as if Sihon should already know this was his uncle's property.

"Yes," Conrad answered. He remained silent to allow Sihon to take in the beautiful pastures and animals grazing in them.

"Wow," Sihon breathed in admiration.

They approached a gate, cement pillars and a cement across the top. The road now led up to an enormous house. Sihon gaped at the splendour of the house, no not a house, a mansion, as Uncle Conrad drove up to the front entrance and stopped. The front entrance was of flailed wrought iron, with a plain pleasant house thatched roof.

"This is your destiny,to inherit all this," Uncle Conrad told Sihon.

Sihon's gaze quickly fell from the heights of the roof tops where he admired the peaked roof that dominated the building. He looked at his aunt then his uncle. "But I'm only here for the summer, Uncle Conrad, I thought."

Help appeared at the car door the instant Conrad stopped at the steps.

"Mr. and Mrs. willks," Uncle Conrad said, "You can take this boy's luggage to his quarters, and show him his room."

"Yes, Mr. Cameron."

"Yes, Mr. Cameron."

This left Sihon free. He looked around at the splendid surroundings as much as he wanted.

He went in through the entrance and stopped. A huge fireplace faced him and on the wall above the fireplace hung a framed picture of waves crashing against a sandy beach. A rose, sand and white coloured rug lay in front of the fireplace. Fire tools hung above the fire pit. A little to his left, in a corner beside the staircase stood a small brown table of the same clouring and material stood a small table. The table was covered with a white lace table cloth. Further back doors stood open, leading out to a balcony.

On the table stood a decoration Sihon had ever seen. It was a doll, made from cloth, stuffed with something and hand sewn together. He also saw some pins of different colours on the table top beside the doll.

What weird decorations, Sihon thought. Someone in the household must like making dolls. Those pins must be used to hold the doll together while it's being sewen together.

To Sihon's left a winding staircase of mahogany, and covered with a thick, plush, cheerful light sand colour carpet,led to an open area upstairs. He could see five doorways. Bedrooms, he imagined. Then his eyes paused as his gaze fell on something strange at the end of the hallway. The other rooms didn't bother Sihon, the door were opened, they seemed bright and full of light and laughter, but the end door was closed tight. Only darkness showed. An evil looking mask hung above the door, gazing with an evil eyes down at anyone who came in through the entrance way. Sihon quickly drew his gaze away from the mask. He had no idea what it was all about. He looked straight ahead. He walked straight ahead across the wide entrance way to the dining-room. He saw a long dark brown wooden table and chairs, cabinets for dishes. He looked behind him to see across the opening the living-room. He walked slowly to the room, gasping at the beauty and size of the room. A window the full length of one wall provided another spectacular views of Georgian Bay,

Sihon strode along and old abandoned logging road on his uncle's property, now lonely and unused. Over one shoulder he'd slung an old backpack, his wet bathing suit inside. His short brown hair was still wet from the water and his face a healthy color from the exercise of swimming.

Coming out of the forest and onto the edge of the pastures closest to the farm buildings, he paused and shaded his eyes and looked off into the distance. Sure enough, far away so he could hardly see them, were Mr. and Mrs. Willks the help he'd seen on arrival, working in the garden. There was a third person. A little girl about eleven. He started at a run across the field towards the farmyard. Once home he hung his bathing suit on the line to dry. Hearing the noise of the line being run out, eleven-year-old looked up.

She said pleasantly. "There you are Sihon. Your parents are here."

"Hi Crystal. Uncle Conrad or Aunt Lillian likely won't be until noon, or later," Sihon said. He hung out his bathing trunks to dry on the clothes line.

"Have a nice swim?"

"I had a wonderful time."

"Was there anyone else at the beach?"

"No, just me." Sihon turned to the two working in the garden. "May I help in the garden?"

Mr. Willks nodded towards one end of the garden. "There's a hoe over there."

Sihon dashed for the hoe and eagerly started digging and hoeing the earth, and separating the harmful weeds from what was intended to grow in the rows.

He stopped his work when he saw his parents come out the back door and start towards the garden, then they stopped in front of him and stood there, preventing him from doing any more work. He flung aside his hoe. He hugged his father, but his mother stood to one side, totally apart from father and son.

"Hi, Dad, Mom," Sihon greeted his parents with obvious joy.

"How long are you here for?'

"We are here for the summer," Mr. Weistien said.

"Come on into the house," his mother ordered.

"Aw, do I have to?"

"Of course you have to," his mother said. "Now, You don't have to be doing this kind of work."

Mrs. Weistien, fussed. "Look at your hands. They are filthy." She waved her hands as if trying to make the dirt disappear. "You wouldn't find your cousin doing this; she's only eleven years old and she has more sense than you."

Mrs. Willks lowered her eyes in shame at Mrs. Weistien's treatment of her son.

Could she not show her son a bit of affection? Mr. Willks wondered.

"This dirt will wash off easily, " Sihon's Dad said. "Leave the boy alone."

Mrs. Weistien waved her hands again, as if to wipe Sihon out of her life, then repeated her earlier command. "In the house."

Sihon turned to his father,"But Dad, I love the vegetable garden and working in the soil."

"It's lovey to the see the results of our efforts in the fall when the vegetables are harvested," Mrs. Willks said. " I love working along side Sihon. I call it our quality time together."

But his Mom wouldn't allow it. Sihon started towards the house. before the boy was out of earshot, his mother turned on Mr. And Mrs. Willks. "I would thank you to not to have any part in my son defying and disobeying me."

"But Mrs. Weistien," Mrs. Wilks began, Mrs. Weistien continued in her hateful way that echoed Conrad's mannerism more and more every day.

"He outright disobeyed me right now when I told him to go to the house."

Mrs. Willks was about to say something, or try to, but Mr. Willks took her by the arm to hush her protests. He drew her to her and held her close as Sihon's mother stalked away.

"What an unhappy woman," Mrs. Willks said.

As Sihon walked he felt angry. When he came to the rough edge the garden soil, he stumbled and fell face first into the soil.

To further his humiliation, Uncle Conrad had come out the back door of the house and approached the group. Uncle Conrad rolled his eyes heavenward. "For Pete's sake. How clumsy can you get? Why was I ever burdened with a nephew like you?"

Sihon sprang to his feet. His uncle's words had cut deeply. He lashed out. "Would you consider me clumsy if I'd your very own flesh and blood-Your son?'

Uncle Conrad didn't reply to this.

Sihon shot at his Uncle, "Unkind, unloving words are all you ever say to me. Is there anything I've done right?"

"Nope."

Hurt more than any other time in his life, Sihon turned and fled towards the house. This time he reached the back door without tripping. He jerked odpen the door then stumbled inside, through the kitchen and into his small bedroom where he flung himself face down on the bed and cried and cried.

Much later, he pushed himself up off the bed and his eyes still red from crying, and his face wet from tears, went into the bathroom. He turned on the water taps and cleaned up. Finished cleaning up, he went to the kitchen. Pulling out a chair he sat down at the table. Through the window he could see Mr. Willks in the field working, attempting to fix a broken fence post all by himself.

Sihon watched as Mr. Willks paused to take a huge handkerchief from his back pocket and wipe sweat from his face, then replace the object in his pocket. Sihon jumped up and dashed outside to where his uncle labored.

He heard Mr. Willks complain, "Oh I'll never get this post repaired."

"I can help."

"What are you doing here?"

"Remember, I'm home for the summer."

"How can I forget?"

"I came to help you put the post in the ground."

"How did you know I needed help?"

"I watched you from the kitchen window. I'll put the brace in place while you straighten up the post."

Sihon almost danced towards the post so excited he was over helping his uncle. Mr. Willks didn't budge.

"It won't work. The cow and her calf will have to stay in the barn for another night. "I'll get someone else to fix the fence."

Sihon said confidently, "We can fix this post together."

Mr. Willks said, "I said it won't work."

"Why?"

" For one thing, you aren't supposed to be out here working. Come on.."

Uncle Conrad came out of the house and joined Sihon and Mr. Willks.

"This is the second time you were told not to do the work around here," Uncle Conrad said.

"I'm going back to the house," Mr. Willks said.

Uncle Conrad watched him go, then turned to his nephew,"What difference does it make now. It's too late."

Sihon disagreed. "It isn't too late."

His uncle said firmly, "Yes it is. While you were with the Asquinns, they said your behavior was appalling. You have such a capacity for getting into trouble, Martin or Audrey Asquinn doesn't even want you around."

This statement stunned Sihon.

"Why would Martin, or Audrey or any of the five girls say that? I loved living there and they , at least, love me."

"Yes I suppose it is possible."

"You think you should give up this farm just because I'm not interested in running the casino. I'd rather farm."

His uncle disapproved. "But I don't think you should run this farm.

I'm selling it and you won't be getting any further compensation from me, or your parents."

"You blame me for hating gambling and all it involves. You really hate me for that don't you Uncle Conrad." Sihon reached out and touched his uncle's shoulder, but the man only shuddered.

"Yes I do. Living with the Asquinns has ruined your desire to operate a paying casino. I intend to keep you here and change that. You are Grant Nigel Weistien the Second' You are not named after that awful name, Sihon Asquinn."

Sihon's uncle started towards the house, now lit up in the inside with electric lights.

"I really want to be a farmer, Uncle Conrad," Sihon called after him.

Sunday turned out to be a glorious, clear summer day. Sihon just returned from Sunday School and Church with Mr. and Mrs. Willks. He returned to his room and had just finished changing from his Sunday suit into regular clothes when there was a knock at the door.

"Come in."

Crystal stepped lightly into the room. "Hi."

"Hi Crystal."

"My, you sound cheerful. Where have you been all morning?" Crystal asked.

"At church," Sihon said.

"Church?" Crystal almost chocked on the word.

"Sure. I went with the Willks."

"Daddy needs some help repairing the garage roof. Why don't you come along and help-Mom and I are helping him."

Sihon jumped to his feet, glad of the opportunity for something to do, glad of the chance to get outside and breath some clean, fresh air.

"All right, all right," he agreed and followed Crystal downstairs and outside to the garage.

"We're all here now," their Mom said.

"Let's get going," Uncle Conrad said. "Lillian dear, you and Crystal and I will climb onto the roof and place the shingles where they are needed."

Sihon couldn't hide his eagerness. "What about me? What can I do?"

Uncle Conrad only looked annoyed, but he handed his nephew a bundle of nails. "Stand near the top of the ladder and hand out these as needed."

Soon the pounding of nails filled the air. All went smoothly, and they were almost finished the job when, as he handed his uncle the last of the nails, his hand started to slip. He did his best to hang onto the bundle, but lost the battle and the nails fell from his hands and scattered all over the roof, and tumbled to the ground. Then, he felt dizzy and the next thing he was falling backwards, then he felt his body crash into the ground below. His aunt, uncle and cousin were at his side in an instant.

Crystal helped him to his feet. "Are you all right?"

"I'm okay."

"Do you hurt anywhere?"

Sihon shook his head.

"You shouldn't have been up there on that ladder in the first place," Mrs. Cameron scolded.

"Yes, Aunt Lillian."

Uncle Conrad rolled his eyes heavenward. "Why was I ever saddled with a child like you?"

"He wanted to help, Mom, Dad," Crystal said.

"You could have given him something different to do besides climbing a ladder," Crystal pointed out.

Uncle Conrad argued. "He simply was not watching what he was doing, and slipped."

Sihon stared down at his toes in embarrassment. Crystal, also embarrassed for her cousin, stared at the ground. Sihon never in his life felt so hurt and humiliated. Crystal reached out and lightly touched her cousin's shoulder. Sihon merely shook her hand off. With his face flushed he put one hand over each ear.

"Stop it! I hate it when you argue about about me front of me as if I weren't even there. Why can't you forgive me?"

One morning a week later, Sihon rose up from his bed earlier than usual. He dressed, carefully opened the door to his room, peeked out into the corridor. Empty. Sihon opened the door far enough to let his slim form slip through, then carefully closed the door behind him. Silently he crept along the plush carpet towards the end room. When he got there he found a scarlet curtain covered the opening to the stairs leading up to another level. The imprint of one sword was sown into the material.

Sihon pushed back the curtain. He jumped from the noise the curtain made moving across the rod. Sihon discovered a staircase led even further upwards, upwards to the half story. Nervously he glanced over his shoulder to see if anyone had discovered him. Why did he always feel, in this house, that he was being watched?

Not seeing anyone, Sihon started up the stairs. At the top was only one room. Sihon stepped into the room. Immediately in front of him was an alter. Not much else beside pictures on the wall. Framed picture caught his eyes. He moved closer and peered at the pictures through the dimness. He guessed they were all pictures of the family. He did not recognize anyone until he came to the name **ARTHUR KONRAD CAMERON THE FIST, AND BRIDE, LILLIAN.** Sihon knew this would be Conrad's parents, and that Arthur was only his father's stepfather. Next was the picture of Conrad with the inscription, **Conrad Arthur Cameron the Second, and bride Lillian** Coming to the next picture, he suddenly felt chilled. The picture was of his father and a woman. He didn't recognize the woman. He read the inscription underneath. **Nigel Weistien and bride, Patrica. Sihon shivered.** *This woman in the picture looked nothing like the woman with his father now. The woman with his father now was not his mother. He knew that.*

Feeling chilled to the bone, Sihon quickly turned and fled from the closet like room. He felt closed in. He ran down the stairs as fast as he could, along the hall and down the stairs to the first floor and outside. He came out of the house onto the deck and picked a chair at the table where his aunt, uncle, Crystal, and parents sat eating breakfast. Nigel smiled pleasantly at his son, but there were no expressions of joy at seeing him from the others.

Sihon knew Uncle Conrad and his father were half-brothers, their father Arthur Cameron. Their parents had left the half-brothers on their own a lot, so engaged were they in raking in money and wordly possessions. The boys were left to raise themselves. They clung to each other for comfort, therefore were bound to each other for life. Sihon's father was more mild mannered than his brother.Uncle Conrad, as his ancestors before him, scorned the beliefs of the Asquinn family and what Pastor Asquinn preached and taught.

Sihon was more subdued than ever, a premonition over took him that he hadn't joined these people to be given good news.

Uncle Conrad began. There was no easing into the subject. He simply dived right in.

"Sihon, you are being sent back to Forest Lake and your beloved Asquinn."

Chapter Three
Sent Back To Forest Lake

Uncle Conrad's words shocked Sihon. He looked at his father, hoping he would explain.

"You didn't want to go inside the other night, did you, Sihon? even though it was almost dark,"

Uncle Conrad said.

Sihon didn't answer right away then he said almost in a whisper. "I love the land; for the freedom of open spaces and I long to be able to work the land." *He stopped himself from telling Uncle Conrad he didn't want to go inside because inside evil filled every cranny. Evil stifled his breathing.*

"There is only one way we will agree to keep you here," Uncle Conrad said.

"How?" Sihon asked. Already suspicious. He looked to his father one more time for help. Mr. Weistien looked him in the eyes and smiled.

For the first time in his thirteen years Sihon felt like he might be on the same page as at least one member of his family. Then his happy bubble burst.

"Farms aren't really paying off these days anyway," Uncle Conrad said. "With floods, droughts and grasshopper plagues, and very little compensation farmers are quitting and moving to the city."

"But that hasn't happened in this area," Sihon pointed out. "Farmers are looking forward to a bumper crop for the next few years."

"They thought that last year," Uncle Conrad said.

"An early snowfall prevented farmers from getting onto the land and harvesting those bumper crops. The crops they did get off lessened in value the later the season grew," Sihon said

"That's true," Uncle Conrad agreed reluctantly. "I didn't know you knew so much about what's going on in farming."

"But none of those named natural disasters have occurred here and we will never know if it would," Sihon said. "This farm is on rich agriculture land. I could have provided a good life for my family. Not as lavish a life as money from the casino would provide, but enough to provide."

"If you want to farm so bad, you can farm this land," Uncle Conrad said. "That's the only way you will remain here."

What? Sihon thought, he didn't want to visit these folks in the first place. He looked at his father. His father lowered his gaze to the floor. What's the matter with him? Is he trying to tell me something?

"Your offer is tempting, Uncle Conrad. I don't want to spend my life here. I'll go back and live with Martin and Audrey. I'm not a part of the Cameron family. I won't even call you uncle anymore."

He heard an audible sigh from his father and a smile lit up the man's face.

Conrad's features contorted into rage. "Pack your suitcases and I'll take you to the casino right away."

Sihon looked to his father for help. "Dad, the train doesn't leave for the north and Forest Lake until nine in the evening!"

"Tisk, tisk," his mother said.

"Why do you have to take him to the casino now at eight in the morning? Crystal questioned.

Her father said cruelly, "Because the rest of us will be too busy this evening to drive him. Don't you realize evenings are the best business hours for the casino? Now don't ask any more questions, little girl."

Sihon felt pity for the girl. Crystal's face contorted as if she was about to cry because of her father's sharp tone and uncaring words. But she held back her tears.

"Dad can drive me this evening," Sihon said. "Can't you, Dad?"

Mr. Weistien said nothing. He avoided looking at his son.

Please," Sihon pleaded.

His father remained silent.

"But what will he do all day?" Crystal said.

"There's lots to do in the city. There's tour buses and all kinds of tours to keep you occupied until your train leaves, and you could hang around the casino- maybe get to like what you see."

"Never! I won't go on any train tours."

"Why not?"

"I'm afraid I'd get lost somewhere and never find my way back in time to catch my train up north."

"Hummph," his father snorted.

"I'll need money."

"Please don't rob any banks," Conrad pleaded. He took a roll of bills out of his pocket and slapped some money down on the kitchen table in front of his nephew. "Now let's get going. I have obligations this morning. I'm certain there will be someone to drive you to the train station when the time arrives."

His father had given him plenty of money to buy a sleeping coach, and his uncle had given him even more.'

Alone in downtown Toronto, and in Conrad's casino, Sihon went off to wander the enormous halls of the mammoth building all by himself. Time and again he looked at a large clock above , only to realize the hands had ticked away only a few minutes since the last time he'd checked.

He noticed the game room set off to one side in one of the corridors. Fingering the bundle of money in his pocket, he wandered inside.

The room was big and beautiful, carpeted throughout, with lots of windows up high through which beams of sunlight shone through. There were rows upon rows of games, none of which Sihon was familiar with.

He stopped by one and fingered the levers; for an instant or two he resisted the urge to play, but then the desire got too strong and he gave in. Pulling out some money, he went for some change and his playing began. At noon he got some sandwiches and a soft drink from a machine. That was his lunch, then he started playing again. The afternoon went by more

quickly than the morning had, and the evening. He glanced at the clock high on one wall and discovered it was already seven o'clock pm.

"Two more hours to go," he said. By now he'd made friends with a group of young people his own age and all were having a great time at the gambling games. "I have plenty of time to win back the money I lost."

He reached into his pocket, but discovered all the money his father had given him was gone.

"Are you going to play or not?" one boy asked him. He was eager to get another game started.

"Naw," replied Sihon

His friends snickered. Sihon didn't pay them any attention. He walked away. He'd tasted of trying to acquire a lot of money at one time. It's just like going to church in Forest Lake had taught him. He had lost a substantial amount of money. Whatever good thoughts he may have had about gambling quickly drained from him.

"Grant Nigel Weistien the Second; The kid whose Uncle owns just about every games house in the city says he's out of money," mocked one boy.

"Mr. Cameron owns this casino," another in the group said.

Sihon turned and walked back to the group.

"Your family's always written about in the social pages of the city newspaper," one girl said. "It was in the news, Conrad Arthur Cameron the third had a visitor home. It was their nephew, Grant Nigel Weistein the second. It's all in that paper over there on the bench."

Sihon's stomach felt like led and he went weak all over as he walked walked over to the purple cushioned and chrome seats and picked up the Toronto Star. He felt as if he would throw up as he looked at the picture of himself looking back at him from the printed page.

He threw the newspaper back on the seat.

"My name is Sihon Asquinn," he told his friends.

He turned and ran the other way.

Is he that easily recognized? he asked himself

I seemed like an eternity had passed to Sihon since he'd seen his Dad at nine O'clock this morning and eaten. How was he to buy food once he boarded the train? How was he to get to the train station? He didn't have any money. How was he to buy a ticket to board the train? Conrad had said someone would be there to drive him to the train station. As the hands of the clock ticked towards seven o'clock, no one showed up

After a lengthy wait, Sihon saw his father approaching through the crowded casino.

Sihon rushed towards him. "Are you here to drive me to the train, Dad?"

"Yes, hurry," Mr. Weistien said. He grabbed a couple of suitcases, leaving the smaller luggage for Sihon. Sihon grabbed the handles of his load and followed his father. The two of them dodged through the crowd and outside to where Mr. Weistien had parked his car.

The two climbed into the car and were quickly underway. Sihon wondered what his father was afraid of. He drove as if afraid someone followed, keeping an eye on him. Conrad? Sihon shivered and turned to watch through the outside rear view mirror. No car appeared to be chasing them.

Mr. Weistien drove in silence through heavy traffic.

"You don't know how happy it makes me to have heard you tell Conrad you don't want anything he has to offer," Sihon's father said at last. "I'm glad to see you going back to Martin Asquinn and his family. Martin is a good man, they will teach you good things. Did you know I spent some time with Pastor Asquinn when I was a kid? Conrad locked me out of the house one cold winter night. I had to sleep under the school house, to keep warm. Then he dragged me back home. Pastor Asquinn and his family took me in and gave me a home after I'd been found. Martin and I became good friends. He led me to Jesus. I did not know how to stand up to Conrad. Stay where you are, son, with the Asquinn family."

Sihon and his father arrived at the Ontario Northland Railroad station.

Mr. Weistien bought Sihon the ticket. He should have enough money for a sleeper car, but Sihon noticed the ticket was for a coach only.

"No matter what happens, son, remember that I love you, and that I always will be your father," he said as he handed Sihon the ticket.

Sihon hugged his father, " If you'd raised me from babyhood, I would have always looked upon you as my father," Sihon said. He sniffed and wiped moisture away from his eyes.

Sihon climbed aboard the Northlander. A huge green and yellow diesel engine pulled at the head of a long line of silver cars with stripes on the sides. Before going into his coach, he turned once more to his father. He saw two men he didn't recognize approaching his father.

"Dad, someone's after you."

Before Mr. Weistien could move, the two men stopped by him, one on either side.

"Son, if we don't meet again on this earth, heed what the Asquinns teach you and what you learn in church," Mr. Weistien called to Sihon. "I'm confident that way we will meet again in heaven."

"I'm confident of that, too," Sihon said.

The train started moving. Sihon hurried to his seat. Out the window he saw the two men with his father walking between them. *Almost like a prisoner being marched back to his cell by prison guards, Sihon thought.*

Sihon sat alone by the window seat, looking out as the train exited the station railroad grounds. His excitement mounted as the engineer blew the whistle and announced they were out of Toronto's city limits. *Headed north, Sihon said. Yes. Soon darkness fell. Except for lights from homes, or a farm, or a small town, he saw only blackness through the windows.* On through the night the train hurtled along the Highway 11 corridor to its goal to a city south of James Bay, Timmins. Sihon would reach his destination of Forest Lake in eleven hours.

The conductor came around then and collected tickets. He lingered over Sihon's admission, studied it carefully, then the boy himself. Sihon's ticket was punched and handed back to him. And the conductor went on collecting, and then a man selling soft drinks and sandwiches appeared. Sihon reached into his pocket for money to buy his supper, then was cruelly reminded that he had gambled all his money away back at the casino. And due to the rush and excitement, he had forgotten to ask his father for more money

The sandwich man stopped by his seat, and asked in a kind voice. "Want to buy some sandwiches, kid?"

Sihon shook his head. The man set two sandwiches and a couple of canned soft drinks beside him. He said before he moved off. "You look as if you can use some food."

Sihon snatched up one sandwich, tore away the plastic wrapping, ate his food, and washed it down with a soft drink.

After that he curled up in his seat and slept. He was asleep most of the night as the train hurtled through the darkness. towards James Bay. He had so much confidence in his parents he didn't even wonder if they had notified any one in Forest Lake of his arrival.

Sihon's eyes opened and he sat up in his seat and looked out the window. Dawn streaked the sky. Soon he would be in Forest Lake. His stomach churned as he wondered what awaited him there.

An entirely new shift of conductors had boarded the train while he'd slept. One entered the car from the opposite end where he sat. His heart slowed as the man stopped by his seat.

"Kind of young to be traveling by yourself so late at night and so far, aren't you?" he asked.

"Someone's meeting me at the station in Forest Lake," Grant said.

"I'm old enough."

"How old?"

"Sixteen."

"Hummph. I doubt that. No use asking you your name, you would give me a false name, anyway."

You sure are a trusting soul, Sihon thought.

The conductor looked at his watch. "We'll be in Forest Lake in an hour."

Sihon nodded. "I know. This isn't my first trip up here."

After several towns and stops the train carried him over the South Blanch River train bridge just a few miles out of Forest Lake. With many whistles and announcing its approach, the train slowed and made its way into Forest Lake. Sihon sat on the side of the coach looking out the window onto Golden Ridge Circle. His coach passed Tadcu and Mamcu's place the manse, Martin's place. Home. But he didn't see anyone stirring.

Probably too early for them all, he told himself. *The twins, along with their father, will be at the train station waiting for me.*

The conductor burst through the door. "Next stop, Forest Lake."

The train screeched to a halt along side the railroad depot. Grant prepared to leave the ca.He looked through the coach window. He didn't see any vehicles, or signs of anyone waiting for him. He noticed, as the conductor helped him off the train, that the man in the baggage car had already neatly stacked his luggage on the depot platform.

The conductor said. "I don't see anyone here."

"Someone will be along soon," Sihon replied confidently.

"Look kid, I don't know what's going on and I can't delay this train long enough to help you more. But if you're smart, you'd go across the street to the police station and ask for help. There's a night shift on duty, the place is all lit up."

"Naw. I'd rather spend the night alone than ask a policeman for help."

The conductor signaled for the engineer to continue, and climbed aboard. The train moved off amongst many whistles and was soon out of sight, leaving Sihon alone with his suitcases in the dark damp night. Feeling worthless, and worse, depressed, he sat on his suitcases, waiting and waiting and hoping, just hoping, that someone would come for him. As time ticked on and no one came, he stirred.

"I wonder where to from here?" he said out loud. "What do I do now? Who's place should I go to? Uncle Conrad was right, Martin and his family don't want me. Why else aren't they here to greet me?"

Then an urging from within stirred him to action.

"I'll go seek out Olvina and her sisters," he said determined. "I will find a welcome there."

He picked up his suitcases and started walking towards east Forest Lake where his home was. His footsteps began to lag as his luggage grew heavier and heavier. He set them down again and sat on one to rest. Again he started feeling sorry for himself.

He asked himself, *Why am I kidding myself? No one wants me even near his or her families. I might as well be dead. I'll kill myself.*

And with that thought in his mind Sihon reached into his side pocket and pulled out a knife he always carried there. He had started the first incision on his wrist and a tiny bit of blood spurted.

The inner urging came again.

I will go to Martin's house. He bent over to pick up his bags then stopped and asked himself.

Why this sudden urgency to get to see Martin, Audrey and the girls? That's the last place I want to go.

But this time Sihon knew he couldn't shrug these urging off as his own thoughts. He hadn't prayed in in a long time, nor had he been encourage by Uncle Conrad or anyone els. He prayed now. He remembered hearing Martin pray during family alter and the power of Pastor Asquinn's prayers whenever he had occasion to pray. It was these patterns Sihon followed now. Un bidden singing came to him. He heard the sweet melody of "God and His Holy Angels."

Sihon knew he was under the care and guidance of his host of guardian angels. Pastor Asquinn often said that all children of God have angels tending them. He prayed in urnest.

Dear God, I know you are there in your splendid home in heaven and have been looking after me during this horrible journey, no, more likely throughout my miserable life, please may I find strength to walk to the twins' with this baggage and may I find acceptance when I do get there.

Suddenly he didn't seem so tired or his suitcases so heavy. Quite a bit of time had passed since arriving in Forest Lake, the sun rose above the treetops by now, but the rays had succeeded in warming up the chill by only a few degrees.

"It's Saturday morning and I'll be lucky if anyone's up," Sihon muttered.

Sihon turned into Asquinn's driveway and made his way to the back door. He set his suitcases down but hesitated ringing the doorbell. Lights weren't in use since the sun was up so high so he could not tell if anyone was up inside.

Probably not, he told himself. I might as well finish what I started earlier. It will serve my stuck up relatives right to find me dead on their doorstep.

But instead he reached out and rang the doorbell. It surprised him when, almost immediately, a face appeared in the porch at the inside door and peeked out the window to see who had rung the doorbell at this early hour. Her eyes grew huge when he saw Sihon huddled on the doorstep. She said and pulled open the door.

Sihon took her looks of surprise as surprise that he'd come back as the family didn't want him. Just like Uncle Conrad told him

"Hi, Phoebe," Sihon said.

Sihon pleaded for all he was worth. "I know you don't think much of me, but, please, I need a place to stay."

"Come on in," Phoebe invited. "Why should I need to ask you? This is your home."

Sihon grabbed his luggage and stepped into the kitchen. The tranisition from the cold morning air outside to the warm inside air made him dizzy and he stumbled a bit as he made his way towards the kitchen chair. As he stumbled, he dropped his suitcases. He looked anxiously around, expecting Martin or Audrey to burst out of their bedroom, clothed in their gowns and slippers and degrade him. But the door didn't open, nor did anyone appear.

"Wasn't anyone aware of change in plans?' he asked

"This is the first anyone here heard about it," Phoebe said.

"My so called family has disowned me," Sihon said. He tried to act as if this didn't bother him, but the break in his voice betrayed him

"You should have a warm bath and thaw out, and change into warm, dry clothes," Phoebe said.

"I will," Sihon promised.

Sihon carried one suitcase into the heated entrance where his bedroom was located by the stairways to the upper part of the house.

By now Phoebe's sisters were awake and downstairs. Martin and Audrey emerged from their bedroom.

"Who does that belong to?' Audrey demanded.

"That suitcase looks like one of Sihon's" Martain said.

Sihon entered the kitchen at that moment, all cleaned up and refreshed.

Martin and Audrey looked at each other.

Again Sihon took the shocked looks were caused because the couple were surprised he'd come back.

"I know you don't want me back," Sihon said in a small voice. "You think I'm a lot of trouble."

"Who told you that?' Martin said.

"Did your father tell you that?" Audrey said.

"Uncle Conrad told me you wanted nothing to do with me," Sihon said.

"Let's have breakfast, then we will talk," Audrey said.

Chapter Four
Messed Up

Everyone dashed into the kitchen. All but Olvina and Cassia noisily sat down at the table.

"I'll help you get breakfast ready, Mom," Olvina said.

"Me, too," Cassia said.

Audrey set the plates of buttered toast and eggs on the table. Sihon dove right in by grabbing a slice of toast and spooning scrambled eggs onto his plate.

He'd spooned a forkful of eggs into his mouth before he looked up. The rest were looking at him, accusingly.

"What?" Sihon said.

"Meals don't start here before grace," Phoebe reminded him.

Sihon looked ashamed. He sat back and waited politely, like everyone else. But, after grace, like the rest of them, he dove right in and started to eat.

Breakfast over with, Olvina pushed back her chair and left the table. Phoebe, Eunice, Cassia and Kathleen followed her.

Sihon started to follow.

"You stay right where you are," Martin told him.

Sihon sat down again.

Once the rest of the children went outside, or to other parts of the house, Martin spoke to Sihon again.

"Now you can explain what you are doing here. We put you on the train only three weeks ago to spend at "Cameron Estate," to spend the summer there."

"We had words. He thinks I'm hopeless, to indoctrinated by church to be of any use to him."

"What else?"

"I won't say another word. I want to talk to Ken."

"I don't think that's possible. He doesn't work weekends."

"Then I won't talk until he comes back on duty."

"All I can do is call Bradan. He's on duty Saturday."

"You mean that's the only way to reach the Chief Superintendent on his days off is through the S/Sergeant?"

"That is the established procedure. Come with me into the front room and I'll see what Ken has to say."

Martin dialed a number and instantly a sparkling voice answered at the other end. "Hello, Asquinn residence. Ken speaking."

"It's me," Martin answered.

"What can I do for you?" Ken asked buoyantly.

"Sihon arrived here an about an hour ago."

"He must have arrived on the early train. Constable Barclay told me, he worked the graveyard shift. He said the train had stopped. What's he doing back here?"

So he already knew he'd come back, Sihon thought. Then he would, his police department always kept well informed.

"That's what I asked him, and he says he won't say a word until he can talk to you."

Ken breathed in a deep, annoyed breath, and said in a tone that he felt no one need be reminded of this, "I don't work Saturdays."

"I know. Sihon won't accept that."

"Okay. Come to my house immediately."

"All right, we'll be there." Martin returned the receiver to its resting-place, and said to Sihon, "Come on. We've been summoned to Ken's residence. It isn't far so we'll walk."

Cassia jumped to her feet, "May I go with you, Dad?"

"Me, too," her four sisters said as one.

Martin looked doubtful, "Maybe not this time, girls."

"Awe, Dad?" five girlish voices begged.

"It will be a chance for the girls to visit with their Aunt Charlotte, honey," Audrey said.

"Come on," Sihon added.

"All right," Martin consented.

When they reached Ken's house, their oldest son, Murray was outside sitting on a bench, enjoying the beautiful morning, his very pregnant wife, Tamara sat on a more comfortable padded wooded chair. Brian, Raymond and Sid played games in another corner of the vast yard. Olvina wondered where Kirk, the second oldest was,The grounds were vast and the house almost a mansion as this was the house Conrad and his half-brother, Nigel, had grown up in. Their father, Arthur Cameron, also got his fortune from gambling casinos. He felt he gave all he owed his sons by allowing them to live in splendour and riches. Otherwise he ignored Conrad and Nigel and let them raise themselves.

Charlotte was with Ken when he answered Martin's knock.

"Good morning," Ken greeted them all.

"Good morning, Uncle Ken, Aunt Charlotte," the couple were greeted plesently by five cheerful girls.

"We came to visit with Aunt Charlotte," Olvina said.

Ken exchanged glances with Charlotte when Sihon did not send forth his usual pleasant greeting along with his foster sisters.

"Come on in," Ken invited.

"Dear, I'll remain outside and visit with the girls," Charlotte said after the visitors stepped inside and before her husband closed the door. Ken nodded and shut the door.

The sound of the door clicking shut caused Sihon's mind to flash back to *Cameron Estate.*

Sihon jumped and yelped, then the grand entrance way at the estate

flashed through his mind. He saw the scarlet curtain blocking

the view of the stairway at the end of the hall, and the decorative sword.

The picture was there for only half a second, but it left Sihon shaken. He leaned against the wall for support. Martin looked at him concerned. He reached out a hand to support Sihon."Are you okay.?"

Ken stepped up to the boy. "What happened? What did you just see?"

Sihon shook his head to clear his thoughts. "Conrad's estate, the upstairs landing and a scarlet curtain hanging at the bottom of a stairs leading up to the third half-story."

Ken rested his hand on Sihon's shoulder. "Let's continue into the living-room."

He guided the boy over to a soft, comfortable looking couch.

"'Sit here." His invitation included both Sihon and Martin.

Ken said when all were comfortably situated. "Sihon, what can I do for you?"

"I want to know if witchcraft is a criminal offense," Sihon said.

"Hummm, withcraft?" Ken said. "It's hardly a police matter. Why do you ask?"

"I'm not sure, but I think Conrad practices it, and I think Crystal is in danger."

"Going by what you told us in the entrance way, that's exactly what he's doing," Ken said. Ken looked at Martin, "The very same curtain that hung on the wall of Conrad's casino here in Forest Lake, before we shut them down. Sihon, was there anything else?"

"A sword decorated the curtain. A wooden sword."

"It doesn't matter of it's real, plastic or wood. It means the same. It sword marks out Conrad's territory for carrying out his rituals. The sword tells the evil spirits this is Conrad's sacred grounds."

"He should be stopped and arrested," Sihon said.

"He should be, but we can't really do anything. Practicing witchcraft is a minor offence with a fine of a mere 500.00."

"To a millionaire like Cornad, that's nothing," Martin said.

Ken chuckled at this. "Neither would a six month jail term."

"So he gets away with what ever evil he's up to?" Sihon questioned.

"We can interfere if he's trying to convince someone of something that isn't true," Ken explained.

"Like a kid's parents don't want or love him anymore?"

"Yes," Ken said.

Something came over Sihon. Suddenly he began to feel irritated. He felt jabs that felt like they came from a pin. He did not want to cooperate with the police.

Ken and Martin looked at Sihon, concern on their faces.

"Are you all right?" Ken asked.

Sihon turned his back on this policeman that was his friend.

"Martin told me you arrived early this morning I took that to mean you arrived on the early train---"

Irritation and the painful jab feelings made Sihon rudely cut Ken off. He turned his back on this policeman that was his friend "That's right, and there wasn't anyone there to meet me. That's what I wanted to talk to you about."

The corners of Ken's mouth curled upwards in annoyance, not accustomed to being interrupted when talking.

Sihon looked distressed. Why do I act like this?

Ken continued as if Sihon hadn't broken in. "So, I checked into it and I was right. I talked to the conductor that worked this morning and he remembers you vividly. He told me you caught his eye immediately, because you were so young and alone. He thought maybe at first you were a run away but changed his mind when you had a legitimate ticket for Forest Lake. He continued to keep a close eye on you."

He burst out with total abandon. "I'm glad someone cared enough to worry about me."

He sat on the couch and his eyes should have been lowered in shame, and his face burning in embarrassment, by the time Uncle Ken came to the end of his account, but not so. He sat unyielding slouched in his chair, eyes smoldering in fury.

Ken stopped talking. Sihon remained silent in his seat.

"Don't you have anything to say for yourself?" Martin said.

Ken breathed a deep sigh of annoyance when Sihon continued to sit silent and uncooperative.

"I have no more questions," Ken told his brother.

"I do if I may," Martin said.

"Certainly you may question Sihon. Go ahead. See if you have any better luck."

Martin got up from his seat and walked over to Sihon. He was tall, and he towered above the thirteen-year-old, and Sihon appeared even smaller by slouching in the chair.

"Why are you hiding your wrists all the time you've been in this house? What did you do between the time you got off the train and finally found your way to the house?"

Sihon only sat there with his arms crossed and his wrists hidden.

"What did you do for two hours?" Ken repeated Martin's question.

"None of your business. I didn't do nothing."

"Show us your wrists, Grant." Martin knelt to be more at the boy's level. When Sihon made no move to comply with his wishes Martin reached out to grab the boy's arms, but Sihon jerked them away and sat on his hands.

Ken got up from where he sat and walked over to Sihon's chair. "I'll just check you over to see what you have for weapons," he said and frisked the boy. It didn't take him long to discover the knife in Sihon's pocket.

"You didn't consider doing anything stupid, did you? We'll take this just to make sure you don't hurt yourself again or anyone else," he stated.

"No. I didn't do nothing. Leave me alone you despicable cop."

To Martin he said. "You're only a civilian, you have no right to question me."

"Yes he does," Ken said.

"You don't know nothing," Sihon raged. "All you, and every officer in the police department, do is his bidding."

There was a sharp intake of breath from Ken and he began in a voice no one ever questioned, not even the other officers in the department.

"This meeting is over with, Sihon.

Sihon challenged arrogantly.

"You can't do that."

Ken said, determined. "I expected cooperation from you. When I agreed to listen to what you have to say and invited you here I wasn't saying I would stay here all morning listening to your impertinence. I thought you had something to say."

"So did I," said Martin. "Sorry."

"Go home, Sihon."

Sihon's words spit out forth from his lips in a manner he didn't know he was capable of, and hadn't been before his visit with Conrad. He didn't have control over his tongue. "I haven't unpacked them after arriving this morning,"

Ken followed Sihon and Martin outside. Olvina, Eunice and Brian, along with Aunt Charlotte, waited in the yard.

Ken indicated to Martin that he was to follow him to shade under some near by trees. Sihon remained where he was.

Ken began, "Martin, it's getting clearer to me that cousin Conrad is controlling Sihon at a distance."

""But how?" Martin asked.

"Easy. Through a voodoo doll."

Martin nodded, "Sihon's said he's spotted at least one at the estate." "All Conrad has to do is talk to the doll as if he were talking to Sihon himself, and jab the doll with pins. I believe he wants Sihon to get to like the idea of inheriting his billions. When Sihon made it plain he doesn't want anything to do with his inheritance, Conrad sent him back here."

From where he sat on the steps, Sihon sneaked a peek towards, Ken and Martin. He saw Martin glance his way, then back at Ken. *They're talking about me, Sihon thought. Martin's saying he and Audrey don't want me around anymore.*

"Let me guess," Martin said, "His desire is to make Sihon so obnoxious to us that we decide we don't want to raise him after all, and send him back to Conrad and his bunch."

"That's right," Ken said. "Now that Conrad's trying to set Sihon against you and your family, this is truly a police matter."

Ken, started back towards the house, Martin at his side, and stopped by Sihon.

"Sihon, you gave me enough information and we will investigate."

"We want to walk with Sihon," Olvina said then noticed the expressions on three faces. "That is if it's all right." She concluded the meeting had not gone well.

Martin looked at his elder brother.

"Sure. You kids walk home together," Ken said.

Once Ken was out of earshot, Olvina turned to Sihon.

"How was the meeting with Uncle Ken?"

Sihon said tonelessly, "Okay. Ken is a jerk."

Martin's lips tightened. "You are getting to be an arrogant jerk! You really blew that meeting, didn't you? Can't you hold that tongue and be nice to anybody?"

Sihon remained silent.

"You've picked the wrong man to tangle with this time," Martin told the younger boy.

"Who does Ken think he is?"

"He's the law in Timiskaming District," Martin reminded the boy. "Ken never backs down from a challenge, and he always emerges from a scuffle unscathed. Older men than you have found this out sordidly."

"What does sordidly mean?" inquired Sihon

Sensing an argument between Sihon and their father, Olvina looked at Eunice and indicated she should follow her.

"Where are you going?" Martin called after her.

"To Trevor's house."

Trevor's mother, Faith Asquinn married Bradley Olverton. Trevor had an older brother, Guy. The Olverton family lived on the other side of the ridge the church stood on, on the corner of the main road that ran through Forest Lake and Wild Rose Lane, a still gravel part of the road that continued into the forest beyond the village. Olverton's also lived kitty corner across the road from Eric and June.

"I'm coming," Eunice said and followed.

Before they got too far Sihon said, not as if he appreciated the girls' company, but more as if it was his birthright for them to have accompanied him home. "Thanks for the company, Olvina, Eunice.".

Olvina or Eunice didn't even acknowledge she'd heard Sihon's thanks, but instead continued running towards Trevor's house.

Martin continued "Conrad thought he had all the troops on his side when he tangled with Ken."

Sihon said, interrupting Martin, "It was him that shut down Conrad's gambling casino? I thought as much."

"Yes it was."

"What's all this got to do with me and my future?" Sihon said, cutting Martin off once more.

Martin continued, ignoring Sihon's rude disruptions.

"Bradan was out west and Ken the only policeman here in Forest Lake. The casino was located by the junction of the highway leading into Forest Lake and the Trans Canada Highway."

"But that's Highway Gas Service Station now," Sihon said, surprised. "It's a busy stretch of highway; Conrad would get business from travelers traveling north, south and from all the little towns for miles around."

Martin clarified further, "Gambling got so bad that teen-agers were drawn in and spent whatever allowance they had. I remember it all so well. We've been told the story so many times it's almost as if we lived the times. After gambling all evening, a lot of kids' grades started to suffer and kids drop out of school. Fathers used whatever money they received from government checks to gamble instead of buying food and clothing for their families. This included school lunch money."

"Sounds like a real mess." Sihon said. His normal mild mannerism had not returned.

"Gambling started drawing kids away from church on Sundays," Martin continued. "But Conrad didn't care. All he was interested in was the money he was racking in. Residents of Forest Lake put Ken under a lot of pressure for a long time to shut that evil place down; and he did."

Sihon knew what Martin had said about Conrad not caring about anything but pulling in the money to be true. His mind went back to the morning his Dad had put him on the train to some north. He had talked to him as if he were in the way of him earning money and couldn't wait to get him out of the way.

This memoery increased his agitation.

"He went in there and with the help from the Lakeview OPP, and God's help, came out of that conflict victorious. Mr. Cameron tried opposing him but in the end had to flee."

Sihon's eyes went dark, even his face darkened and his features changed. He clutched at his elbow. If Ken had witnessed this, he would be reminded of Conrad, when they were boys in school. Conrad, the high priest of evil, looked his role in every way. Sihon clutched at his shoulder and said just as evil. He's felt a sudden jab of pain so intense he almost cried out.

"Are you okay?' Martin asked. He reached out to touch Sihon, but he jerked away,"Of course, I am. Why wouldn't I be?What a bunch of senseless talk. May I ask what happened next in this fantasy story?"

"He packed up his family and belongings and literally ran away from Ken," Martin went on. His voice had risen. "Ken chased him half way to North Bay in the police car. Conrad hasn't been around here any after that. He stays down south where he's set up his evil gambling again. There's Bradan and Constable Barclay. Don't look for Sympathy from those two, Sihon."

Sihon said, scorn back in every fiber of his being, "I have no idea what you're talking about."

Sihon guffawed off all warnings. "I'm not afraid of any police, Chief

Superintendent, or not. What can he do to me?"

Sihon and Martin had arrived home. Audrey was outside on the back step shaking out a rug when the two rounded the corner of the house. Martin and Sihon were arguing. They were shouting back and forth at each other. She watched in amazement as Sihon, his face distorted with anger,strode past the steps.

"Sihon, you are grounded," Martin shouted. Sihon kept on towards the woodshed.

"Dinner is ready, Sihon," Audrey called after him.

"I'm not hungry," Sihon replied.

instead of going inside, Sihon went to the woodshed, empty of it's winter wood supply. He found a block of wood and sat down. He thought.

"I know I'm the villain and Ken Asquinn hailed as the hero again," acknowledged Sihon. *"After all hadn't the conductor asked if I was a runaway? I'm the one to come out of this pointless conflict scorched. How long will it take me to win back my good name and the trust of these citizens of Forest Lake? So far this summer is a disaster. I'm turning all those I love against me. Martin, Ken, Audrey, the girls. Why? I can't understand what's come over me and how will I continue?*

His thoughts flashed back to Conrad's house; the exterior, the tall tower dominating the center of the building, arched windows, corners that pointed upwards and spiked railing on the roofs. The voodoo doll and pins?

Chapter Five
Alone In The Woods

The rest of the family had eaten and the girls had washed up the dishes when Phoebe came out and stood on the dirt, wood chip filled woodshed floor, close to Sihon. Dusk was falling and Phoebe could barely make the boy's form in the deeper shadows inside the shed. A short time later her four sisters came out of the house and joined her. The soft sound of waves slapping along the shoreline soothed Sihon and he relaxed for the first time since his talk with Olvina at the start of the summer. From the public beach far down the shore came the sound of music blaring, and laughter, which drew Sihon's attention immediately.

"Another party?" he said. "I wonder if it's teen-agers? I wonder what fun I'm missing by not joining them?"

The five sisters were shocked at the degree of interest in his tone as he spoke the words.

Wapinkino came around the corner of the house, went by the steps and joined Phoebe and Sihon. Wapinkino glanced at Sihon as he did so.

The dark skinned youth noticed Sihon's face resembled a thundercloud.

Sihon felt jealous because Wapinkino should feel so at home around Martin and the family. Unfamiliar feelings seized Sihon. He tried shaking them off, but they gripped him and held him prisoner. He felt like getting up and shoving Wapinkino off his chair and wiping that smug look off his face. He knew better than to do mean things like that. Instead he sprang to his feet and started towards the driveway.

Phoebe called after him, "Where are you going?"

Sihon didn't answer. He knew if he stopped to explain, Martin would see him and haul him back in no time and not allow him his freedom. Instead he kept going. "How many places are there to go in this cow town?"

"Don't stay away too long," Phoebe said. "It will soon be bedtime. Church tomorrow."

"Yeah, yeah," Sihon said, but continued walking straight towards the public beach, where he took this to be the place where the music came from. He walked along the tracks and even before he got within a quarter of a mile of the public beach, rock'n roll music reached his ears. It was loud music and Buddy Holly almost screamed, the words unclear. At least they would have been to adult ears. To Sihon and other teen age crowds, the words and music caused them to respond and join parties all over the world. Sihon suddenly felt he was no different. Couples danced to some loud music coming from a boom box. Sihon walked up to a girl he'd talked to on the last day of school."

"I remember you. You're Sihon."

"And you're Vanna. We talked the last day of school. You also board with Mr. and Mrs. Asquinn during the school year."

" These are my friends, Cora, Kirby. Care to dance with me?"

"Sure. Bedtime!" Sihon scoffed. "What squares that Asquinn Family are."

Vanna looked at the sky and then all around. "The sun's still shining. We have till morning to party."

Sunday afternoon, the telephone rang. Sihon started to reach to answer it but Martin stopped him. "I'll answer that."

A few minutes later he hung up and turned to Sihon. "That was Guy Olverton, Trevor's older brother. He's getting together with a carload of cousins and going up north to visit an uncle. He wanted to know if you're interested in going. The girls, Trev and Wapinkino have already agreed to go."

"But I don't want to go visiting I want to swim!"

"But you are not, I repeat are not going swimming."

"Why not? My parents would let me. I went swimming whenever I wanted to at home."

"Then your parents are fools. You know there are rules in this household and you have been grounded. I told Guy you and the rest will be ready when he gets here in fifteen minutes."

Sihon was furious Martin would make a decision like that without first consulting him. He didn't stop to realize he should be going out with kids his own age.

"Oh all right," murmured Sihon. "If I have to."

Audrey approved. "That's good. It's nice to see you're taking an interest in getting out more. Since you arrived back, you have not exactly been social. You've changed."

A little while later Sihon stopped where Martin was seated in the front room. "I'm off."

Martin looked surprised. "I didn't hear a car." He looked out the window. "No one is there yet."

"I'll wait outside for them."

Martin looked dubious. "Whatever you prefer. Have a good time."

Sihon went outside to the front lawn. No one could see him from the front room window, so he didn't have to worry about Martin looking out the window and discovering what he was up to, he thought rebelliously. Just then a cream colored car turned into Asquinn's driveway with the top down. Three teen-agers listened to a musical tape playing Christian music ever so softly. Bradan had joined together with Ken as a duet. Bradan had thought up the nam "The Gospel Singing Cops" for the duet. They sang together in prisons, churches, and put together tapes. In addition to singing, Ken and Bradan played fiddle music. The tune Sihon had just heard was them playing their signature tune.

Sihon peeked through the hedge surrounding the front lawn. He guessed the car to be Guy's because he knew him from church. Guy drove now.

Remaining hidden in the dark shadows of the bushes, he watched as Olvina, Cassia, Phoebe, Kathleen Eunice, and Wipinkino, bounced out of the house and joined Guy, Trevor and Lyle in the car. Sihon noticed that Olvina spoke to Guy but the older youth shook his head. Olvina looked around, puzzled, then turned to Phoebe.

"They're likely wondering where I am," Sihon chuckled.

Shortly Guy backed out into the street and drove away. Sihon smiled. He didn't go back into the house.

Still hidden, Sihon noticed Martin round the corner of the house, start across the front lawn' then suddenly stopped. Sihon's heart skipped a beat thinking he had been discovered. He hardly breathed, afraid he would be found hiding behind the shrubbery. Instead Sihon went back into the house through the front entrance. Quickly Sihon rose to his feet and started running. He flew along the road for some distance before he played out, then he walked, not knowing where the road would take him.

A voice spoke beside him. "Hello."

Sihon's head jerked around. The boy's face standing beside him was familiar and he placed him immediately. He was a handsome youth with short brown hair and brown eyes. At his side sat a huge gray and white dog.

"You are Owen Winschell," Sihon said. "We see each other at school at church."

Sihon looked questioningly at the big grey dog.

"This is my dog, Snow Queen. She's a Canadian Eskimo Dog."

Sihon hoped the guilt he felt didn't show too much. He wondered if Owen knew about the trip north to visit? He should, members of the small church always knew what other members were doing. If he did, he didn't say anything about it to him.

"Oh."

The next words slipped out before he could stop them. Suddenly he didn't have control over what he said. "It would be nice to be in the cool water!"

He quickly caught himself and explained. "Swimming is one activity I love; I miss it greatly."

"You do get to swim while staying with your cousins."

"I haven't been in the water much. Often I've craved to cool off in the lake."

Owen looked puzzled. "But why wouldn't you get to swim? Trevor and Wapinkino swim a lot."

Sihon didn't care to offer further explanation. He shook himself and said, "Never mind."

"I imagine you miss home too. Hummmmm, I thought you *were* home for the summer."

"Back home I had been able to take a cool dip whenever I felt like it. Dad didn't care."

Owen looked at Sihon strangely. He said. "Guy Olverton mentioned going to invite you and some other kids to go visit an uncle up north this afternoon. Guy and his party left over an hour ago."

Anger roiled up within Sihon. He remarked. "Does everyone think I'm not capable of entertaining myself?"

Owen shook his head and said, "I must get back to my chores."

"And I must get on with what I was doing," said Sihon. Owen started towards the driveway up to his house expecting that Sihon would follow, but Sihon had taken off at a run in the opposite direction.

Owen called after him. "Asquinn's place is that way."

Sihon didn't hear him and kept on running.

On past the bridge he kept running and soon found himself on an old road, which was nothing more than wheel tracks etched in the moss and sand with the thickest of forest growing on either side of the tracks. Alone, and free from restraint, he ran not watching where he put his feet. After awhile he wandered off the tracks and came out on the riverbank again. The bank were lower here; the current swift and strong and a sandbar had formed in the middle. The water churned and foamed high around it forming a pool between the bank and sandbar. The pool looked deep but the current didn't appear swift and dangerous, like further out. The placid waters of the pool provided an excellent place to swim. Sihon slipped off his sneakers and socks, and then waded into the stream in his shirt and jeans. He only intended to get his feet wet, but now was his chance. He wanted to get even wetter. So he waded out into deeper water and plunged in. he appreciated the cool water as it closed around him. How refreshing the water felt.

The sun dipped behind the treetops. The shadows lengthened. Sihon realized he should start back to home without delay. He returned to his shoe and socks and slipped into them, then looked around. He couldn't remember which way led home. He started walking and tramped for a long time, but didn't come to the edge of the forest where he entered. The evening advanced. The sun sank lower, the air grew cooler and cooler.

Sihon felt uncomfortable in the wet clothes. His wet clothes did nothing to provide warmth.

Birds that made the forest their home sang from their perches in the trees; a red squirrel ran out onto a branch above Sihon's head. It sat there on its haunches, bushy tail curled along its back, scolding him. Sihon did not like the many noises of the forest. It was home to all the animal kingdom and they scared him.

The underbrush became a thick tangled mass of young willows and all kinds of weeds, but Sihon pushed bravely on through the jungle like entanglement. Branches from small trees whipped his face and stung; thorns from raspberry plants as well as wild rose bushes ripped the flesh on his arms and legs, leaving deep gouges as well as shallow scratches. He ignored the pain and blood. All he wanted to do was get back to Martin's place. Martin and Audrey and the girls would be worried about him by now, he was certain.

It was too dark for Sihon to see his way, so he found a tall spruce tree with thick branches that would shed the rain if it happened to storm overnight, and flopped down in the soft earth by its roots- and the tears began to flow. It was completely dark now; a total darkness that seemed alive, pressed on his chest until he could hardly breathe. He felt as helpless as when some classmates locked him in the shed years ago. At first Sihon fell into an exhausted sleep; when he awoke again, he felt the sunshine warm on his cheeks. He sat up and rubbed his eyes. He immediately noticed the utter stillness of the forest. It had rained overnight but had stopped and the clouds had cleared away, the sun shone, soon the grass and underbrush would be dry.

Sihon tried to stand up, but pain wracked his body. His legs and knees ached as well as the side he had slept on during the night; his neck was stiff and sore. He groaned. How could he move let alone find his way back?

Next, he examined his arms and legs. He discovered an extra deep gash in his left ankle. He studied the jagged would and decided it needed attention immediately. Looking around to find out what he could use as a healer, he noticed Poplar trees growing in abundance here, and not far away stood a stand of Birch trees. He knew the under bark of the Birch acted as excellent painkiller and the sap from the Poplar a balm for his burning scratches. Sihon stood up, and with great effort limped towards the Birch trees. He took out his knife from a side pocket, started tearing away at the outer bark. Half an hour later he felt ready to start the quest back.

He started walking. Although he had cleaned and doctored the wounds as best as he knew how, he was quickly reminded of them. They itched and burned and were stiff and sore. He couldn't linger any longer; he had to continue home. And then he heard a noise in the underbrush. Holding his breath, and with heart thumping, he heard it again, this time much closer. He froze in one spot. The rustling was some animal moving around and whatever it was, it was coming towards him! And then a large wolf like animal pushed its way from some underbrush and made its way towards him. Frightened, Sihon tripped and fell backwards and lay on the ground, unable to get any part of him to respond to his brain. Extra loud panting reached his ears as a huge furry animal plodded up to him and stood over him. And then another form pushed itself into sight from the tangle of underbrush.

"Snow Queen what have you found there?" a young voice called. "Snow Queen, get away from there."

The animal moved away from Sihon, but still frightened the voice might belong to someone that would harm him, Sihon remained huddled on the ground.

He heard a voice say, "Sihon," but he didn't look up.

"Sihon it's us."

Sihon looked up between his arms and saw his cousins, Wipinkino and Owen standing in front of him. Among them sat Snow Queen.

Olvina greeted him brightly. "Hi."

"You missed a great time visiting yesterday afternoon," Phoebe said.

"Where were you?" Kathleen wanted to know.

"Too bad Mr. Asquinn made you stay home," said Owen.

Sihon didn't say anything.

"You're up bright and early exercising," Wipinkino said.

Trevor asked, "Where are you headed now?"

"Home," Sihon said. "I've all the exercise I want for awhile."

"We'll walk with you," Cassia said.

"The only thing is I'm lost," Sihon said. "I don't know which way is home. Standing on the riverbank has confused me for a moment or two. I can't remember if the current flowed into or away from the lake."

"All rivers flow north into James Bay, but at this point, rivers flow south and empty into the St Laurence River, so the current flows into Lake Forest," Wipinkino said. "We won't get anywhere by following the river. We'll have to find the road."

Sihon's sores resulted in slow progress. Pain all through his body reminded of his cuts and scratches.

"Let's stop and rest," Olvina said and guided Sihon over to a fallen tree trunk and set him down. The rest found another nearby tree for a seat, while Olvina made herself as comfortable as she could on a low rock and Trevor found a tree root.

"Mom will know how to take care of those silly scratches," Eunice said.

"I can't help but think of your Mom and Dad," Sihon said.

"Why so concerned about them all of a sudden?" Olvina said.

"Why didn't I listen to your Dad and go with Guy? This brings back memories of stories my cousin Crystal told me. Lots of times she went go to the bus stop, which wasn't very far away from our house, but hidden by some trees. She carried her lunch box and books and go to the stop like she normally would, but instead of getting on the bus, she'd hide her books and taking along her lunch kit, have a much more fun day playing in the woods. Then at four O'clock she'd arrive home at the normal time with her books and empty lunch kit. Always by the time she reached home her teachers would have called her Mom to ask why she wasn't at school. By the time she reached home she always knew Crystal been truant. Mom would scold her but never really punish her. Her Dad never cared enough to say a word about it to her. But will your Dad ignore it? Why am I acting like Crystal?"

"Probably not," Wipinkino said causing Sihon to smile at this.

"Let's get going," Sihon said, and the group pressed on.

A mile further on, Sihon paused to listen, "We must be getting close to the edge of Forest Lake or coming to a farm. I hear dogs barking."

"That's my place we're coming to," Owen explained. "Snow Queen is only one of many sled dogs we have."

"Oh," Sihon said, disinterested.

Then they were out of the thick woods. The trees thinned out and were almost park like along the bank of the river, and the area surrounding Winschell's property.

Sihon struggled to keep going, but had to stop for another rest. They'd had rested for only a few moments when Sihon spotted a black and white police car coming towards us.

"There's Ken and Bradan," he said.

"Are you sure it's Uncle Ken?" Olvina said. "Remember he's teamed Uncle Bradan up with Constable Barclay."

"I see Uncle Ken in the passenger seat and Uncle Bradan driving," Trevor said. "I can see them both plainly."

"Great," complained Sihon.

"And I can see a third man in the back seat," Wipinkino said.

"That's likely Constable Morley Barclay," Cassia said. "He's been with the department for only three months. The three of them work together."

"Doesn't Bradan mind?" Sihon said.

"He's not complaining," Olvina said.

"I sure would ," Sihon said. "I wouldn't allow anyone to push me around! I suppose they're looking for me. Well tell them you haven't seen me."

Wipinkino demanded, "Sihon where are you going? Look you silly kid, if you've seen them then they spotted us half an hour before we saw them; it won't do any good to try and hide."

Sihon said rigidly, in a tone the others had never heard from him before. "I don't like cops. They're all a bunch of hypocrites and a lot of them abuse their powers. Why would these two be any different?"

Sihon slid from the rock and quickly hobbled over to a thick stand of young trees growing close to the shoulders of the faint pathway aSjust as the police car drew up and stopped beside where the group of girls and boys rested. Sure enough, three police officers got out of the car. It was Ken and Bradan that walked up to the boys.

Bradan paused to give instructions to the constable. "Go after the kid that ran away." Constable Barclay continued on into the tangle of bushes after Sihon.

It didn't take long for Constable Barclay to return with Sihon limping along as fast as he could ahead of him.

"Put him in the car and wait there with him and make sure he doesn't get away," instructed Bradan.

The Constable ushered Sihon past his friends still perched on the rock, and into the back seat of the cruiser and slid in beside him.

" Who wants to ride in the cruiser ride back with us," Ken. "It's obvious you all can't fit in the back seat."

"I'll ride back, please, Uncle Ken," Kathleen said.

"And me," Cassia said.

"Me, too," Eunice spoke up.

Kathleen reached the car first and slide inside Morley who sat beside Sihon. Cassia followed.

Released from having to ride in the police car, Owen turned and ran across the fields to his home. Olvina, Kathleen, Phoebe, Wapinkino and Trevor started at a run towards Forest Lake and home.

Ken and Bradan climbed into the front seat.

"Where are you taking me?' Sihon said.

"Never mind, just enjoy the ride," Bradan said.

Chapter Six
Secure Again

Braden turned the cruiser around and the drive home started. Ken looked behind him at the back seat and inquired. "What are you kids doing up so early?"

"It isn't early, Uncle Ken," Kathleen answered . "It must be mid-morning by now."

"You might say it's more like Mid-day," Bradan said.

Ken said, "The point I'm making is, it was early when you guys first came out here. Kathleen, your parents told us you and your sisters were gone from home since six this morning. Mr. Winschell wondered why Owen didn't show up for work this morning. "

"Yes, that's right," said Kathleen. "We wanted to see if we could find Sihon. We woke up and, on our way to the kitchen, noticed his bed hadn't been slept in. We enlisted Wipinkino's, Trevor's then Owen's, and even his dog's, help to find him."

In the back seat ,Constable Barclay noticed the scratches and bruises on Sihon's hand and wrists. He studied the them."How did you get those cuts and bruises?"

Sihon answered rebelliously, "I wasn't watching where I was going."

He sat in the back seat rigidly staring out the front window, and then he said.. "I hate cops School children and people around the world are taught in this country the cops are squeaky clean and are the good guys, which never do wrong, their image is always so clean. Yet I know different. Do school kids know cops blow out kids' brains just to avenge the death of one of their own? I've been part of many incidents where the cops aren't so friendly and kind. They harass people no end. Yet the kids are taught that the police are good and the police will do anything to keep this image. Ha! Once a policeman gets into uniform he thinks he's somewhere equal with God."

Kathleen stared at Sihon in disbelief. "That's not our police force.

What would we do without our Ontario Provincial Police? We need them. We could never do without."

"Thank you," the three officers said.

Bradan cast an annoyed look over his shoulder at Sihont. Ken also cast him a black look. Then he turned his attention to Bradan. "Have you ever heard of a suspect blown away for revenge or have you heard of harassment on this force?"

"No, to both questions."

Ken assured the boy. "The officers on my police force don't eliminate those that oppose them. And if I do hear of anything like that then they'll have me to deal with. You're thinking of another organization. Answer Constable Barclay's question."

"I stumbled into a thorny patch of weeds and flowers."

The scratches and cuts were making Sihon queezy. He felt weak and almost toppled over into Kathleen's lap.

"Are you okay?" she said. "Do you need medical attention?"

"I'm fine," Sihon said.

There wasn't much talking after that. They were almost home. They passed the empty house, the first house entering Forest from the east, on past Trevor's place. Bradan guided the cruiser around the corner onto the main road through the village, past Eric's place, around the sharp curve below Golden Ridge where the manse and church were located, drove a little further and turned into Martin's driveway, and parked by the back door.

Sihon didn't thank Ken, Bradan or Constable Barclay for the ride home. He stepped out of the cruiser as if it was his birthright for them to have done so.

Ken stated. "We're walking you to the door."

Tired from the long night in the woods and sore from his wounds,

Sihon didn't argue. Stiffly he got out of the car and started towards the door with an officer on either side of him. His stomach churned nervously when Ken rang the doorbell. He heard the bell ring from deep within the house. Immediately there was movement from inside as someone hurried to the door and the door was unlocked from within and pulled open.

Audrey stood in the doorway. She looked like she had not slept all night, or if she did, she slept in her everyday clothes.

Audrey sighed with relief when she saw Sihon. "Oh thank God you're back!"

Sihon rushed to her and into her arms.

He said, "You look like you haven't slept all night."

Tears pooled in the corners of Audrey's eyes. "I was worried sick about you."

"Who is it?" Martin asked from behind Audrey.

"It's me," Sihon answered.

"We brought him and the girls home," Ken said. "We found them in the woods east of the South Blanche River."

Martin straightened up from welcoming Sihon back with an enormous hug. He said to the three police officers. "Thank you for bringing him, them, home."

"We won't stay," Ken said. He and his men turned and returned to the cruiser.

Audrey turned to Sihon. "You, young man, are a disgraceful sight."

Then her tone softened and she said more gently, "You are going to get cleaned up right away. And those scratches need attention. Upstairs and into the bathtub."

"Yes Ma'am," Sihon said. He sneaked a peak at Martin.

His lips tightened.

He's angry with me, thought Sihon. He's going to scold me.

"Go do what Audrey said," Martin said. "We'll talk later. Everyone is so tired now. We all need a bit of time."

He turned and stalked away.

An hour later, Sihon stood in front of the full-length mirror hanging on the bathroom door, examining the damage the thorns from the rose bushes from the night before had caused. He had bathed and was now fully clothed. Olvina entered the bathroom. She gave the younger boy a gentle shove towards the closed toilet seat. "Sit there, roll up you pant legs. Mom asked me to check if there's any thorn scratches on your legs."

Sihon bent over and pulled up one pant leg. Olvina knelt and looked the leg over, and gasped. "Sure enough, some scratches do need attention without delay" She stood up reached up into the medicine cabinet and took out an ointment container. This she opened and started spreading it on the cuts and other wounds.

Sihon drew in a deep breath and made a face.

"Are you okay?"

"I'm okay. The salve stung at first but now it feels warm and tingly."

Olvina could not hold back her curiosity any longer. "Where were you last night? What happened?"

Sihon groaned. This ordeal was starting to take its toll on him.

"Go away. I suppose your father is angry with me? He will likely harass me and drill me for an explanation."

"Sihon, that is no way to talk about Dad and Mom," Olvina said sharply. "In this household children show respect for their elders."

She paused to dab some more ointment on one of Sihon's scratches. "Mom and Dad were very worried about you."

"Sorry," Sihon apologized none too enthusiastically.

Olvina finished cleansing the wounds and left Sihon alone.

Sihon tip toed to his room. Before going inside he glanced upwards. All was quiet on the level where the girls slept. He imagined the girls were in were in their beds getting a few more winks after their early morning adventure. He turned and retraced his steps back to his room.

Sihon awoke, alone in the room. He pushed back the covers and got up from the bed and moved towards the door. Voices from the kitchen where Martin and Audrey breakfasted reached him . Although he hadn't eaten since the conductor left the sandwiches with him, he couldn't stand the thought of food, so he turned away from the door and hopped back into bed, pulling the covers over him. He didn't even think before drifting off to sleep about how grateful he should be to this family for a cozy bed to sleep in, dry clothes and best of all, warm and caring relatives.

Much later in the day Sihon woke up. He didn't get out of bed immediately, but lay staring at the ceiling thinking. Martin had spoken politely enough to him this morning, but underneath Sihon realized he boiled with fury over his behavior. As he lay alone with his thoughts the need for food suddenly overwhelmed. He sat up in bed. The hands on the clock on the night table beside his bed showed eight-thirty. Wow! Way past dinner time, way past supper. He had slept through the morning, lunch and afternoon, and he had intended to sleep an hour or two only.

Sihon dressed and hurried downstairs. He could hear the family in the front room, listening intently to what Martin taught from the bible resting on his lap.

"May I please have something to eat?".

Eunice, told him, "We're having family devotions now."

"But, Eunice, I'm starved," Sihon pouted. A feeling of irritability came over him.

"Shes right," Martin said.

"You can eat in a minute or two," Audrey said.

Annoyed, Sihon sat down beside Olvina. He couldn't concentrate on what Martin taught. He fidgeted and squirmed. The words slid right over his head. His mind did not grasp the understanding of one sentence uttered that evening. He breathed a sigh of relief at the closing prayer.

"Now you can have something to eat," Martin said.

"Cassia," said Audrey, "there's food for him in the oven. Give it to him, please."

Olvina sprang to her feet.. "I will. Come on, Sihon."

Sihon followed her into the kitchen where she set a plate and cutlery in front of him, and bowls of food. Like a starved animal Sihon piled mashed potatoes, gravy, vegetables and roast beef onto his plate and spooned food into his mouth.

"Did you stop thanking God for that food?" Cassia, who had followed them into the kitchen, asked.

"Huh?" muttered Sihon. He looked at his cousins as if they had no mind at all.

"Oh nothing," Cassia said.

Olvina placed a glass of milk in front of Grant. "Just keep on eating."

Sihon kept on chewing. "I intend to."

Martin joined him at the table just as he finished his first plate of food, so Sihon filled up his plate again and ate slowly. Finished with his second helping he asked if he could have a slice of apple pie.

Martin inquired after Sihon had finished his second dessert. "How do you feel after your sleep?"

"Much better," answered Sihon. Now finished with his pie, he started to stand up. Olvina and Cassia had moved to the living-room.

"Stay right where you are, Sihon."

"But I want to go outside."

"You'll go outside when I'm finished talking to you."

"Great!" Sihon said. "Here comes the lecturing."

He rose to his feet and shoved his seat aside so violently it went flying. The chair landed on its side half way across the kitchen. The noise made those in the living-room cringe.

Sihon dashed for the door. He didn't make the distance. Martin cut him off before he reached the entrance.

"Pick that chair up and put it back where it belongs. And do it properly."

Sihon did what he was told.

"Now sit down. You and I have lots to talk about."

Sihon sat.

"Do you have a reasonable explanation for your behavior last night?"

"I suppose not," Sihon said, flippantly then thought he should add. "I'm sorry."

"I wish I could believe that, Sihon."

"I'm sorry Martin. I don't know what came over me. It's as if something else is controlling me at times."

"Explain anyway. I'd like to hear it. How did you manage to spend the entire night away from home?"

"I was terribly scared and lonely."

"Were you alone?"

"Yes, I was alone."

"Where did you spend the night?"

Sihon stammered, "I wasn't with Guy and the others like I told you."

"Were you alone?"

"Of course I was alone."

Martin reminded him. "Watch your manners. You lied to me when you told me you were going out to wait for Guy and the others. Then deliberately disobeyed me when I told you not to go swimming. You caused Mrs. Asquinn and me great worry when you didn't come home after dark."

Sihon reminded Martin brashly. "It wasn't me who wanted to go visiting in the first place."

"Watch your manners. I won't say it again."

Sihon replied more respectfully. "I met Owen while I was wandering about yesterday afternoon."

"He told me he saw you by the South Blanche River Bridge," Martin said. "His father phoned here to tell us when he heard we were looking for you. We also phoned around to inquire whether you were at other houses. Imagine our surprise when we were told you hadn't been seen all day. Owen admitted he wondered at the time he spoke to you whether you knew exactly where you were. He knew you had been invited out visiting."

Sihon groaned inwardly. He'd been afraid if something like this. Oh well, he thought; better to get this all out in the open.

"Did he mention whether anyone was with me?"

"He said you were alone at the time."

To Sihon the questions seemed to go on and on and on.

I might as well apologize and get this over with; otherwise, I could be here all day, Sihon thought.

"I'm sorry. What I did was stupid and thoughtless and I deserve to be punished." He even managed to get tears to trickle down his cheeks.

"I wish I could believe you. It's late. Go to bed and now and get some rest. You will need to be rested for your police interview tomorrow. Now you can leave the table."

Sihon rose stiffly from his chair and limped towards the stairs in one corner of the front room. Olvina, followed by Cassia, jumped up from where they'd been sitting and appeared in the front room doorway.

"We'll help you to your bed. You look like you won't make it on your own."

Sihon smiled weakly. "I am rather stiff and tired. I felt lots better after my sleep, but I feel tired again."

The girls allowed Sihon to walk ahead of them, but held onto him, guiding him.

Olvina and Cassia turned their backs and held a hand over their eyes while Sihon changed into pyjamas, then both girls helped Sihon climb stiffly into bed and pulled the covers over him.

"I wonder who's going to interview me tomorrow?".

"Why Uncle Ken of course," Olvina said.

Sihon said nervously, "Oh."

Something in the boy's tone alerted the sisters.

"Why, don't you trust him?" Cassia said.

"I'm not sure," Sihon said.

"Make up your mind," Olvina said softly. "If you don't know you will soon learn because after tomorrow he will have a lot to say about your future. Actually, there's three, Uncle Ken, Uncle Bradan, and Aunt Martha.

Sihon shivered and Olvina and Cassia glanced at him curiously. Olvina reached out and touched his knee. "Something's troubling you. Care to tell us?"

"I'm scared. I mean, lately I haven't given anyone here much good to judge me by after what I've done, have I?"

Olvina squeezed the boy's shoulder. "There's a lot to be considered. Don't worry about your past behavior. Just try to be yourself and answer questions as truthfully and naturally as you know how. For that, as Dad so wisely said downstairs, you will need your rest."

Sihon blurted out. "This hamlet is getting to be boring? Not only is Tadcu the pastor but his son, Tim, is associate Pastor and principal of the school, Ken's the police Superintendent and Bradan second in command?"

Cassis gasped at Sihon's words and covered her face with her hands. Olvina stared at him.

"Sihon, living in Forest Lake never bothered you before, and you've lived with us for twelve years."

"Uncle Ken does set awfully high Godly standards," Cassia said.

"And he lives them," Olvina said. "He's a man any kid in Forest Lake and especially his nephews and nieces, should be proud to look up to."

"How am I ever going to live this down with the other kids in this town?" Sihon said.

Olvina tried explaining. "The kids will like and respect you if."

Cassia said, "Let's get some sleep."

"No," Olvina disagreed, "we should say our prayers."

"Prayers?" Sihon repeated as if he had not ever said a prayer in his life. A prayer before bedtime, or any other time, had not been thought of the three weeks he's stayed at Cameron Estate.

The sisters looked at him, appalled.

"Come on," Olvina said.

"Naw," Sihon said.

Cassia knelt by the wooden chair in the room, Olvina knelt at the end of Sihon's bed. Sihon rolled his eyes in disgust, then to humour the girls, went along.

"Please, Jesus," Olvina prayed, "please keep us all safe this night. Amen."

"Amen," Cassia said. Both girls stood up. They looked at Sihon to find he was already asleep.

Cassia led the way to the door. Olvina turned off the light as the girls left the room. Olvina left the door part way open.

'Good night,' she said.

The next morning Sihon moved along the short hall way at police headquarters where he was to be interviewed. To him the hall seemed endless. He walked beside Bradan and on the officer's other side, walked Martha Asquinn Turehue, the public nurse, and married to Bradan. She carried a fat envelope under one arm. On past an office where Constable Braclay sat, a phone receiver to his ear.

"Which office is yours?"

"We're coming to that. It's right across the hall from Ken's. Here we are."

Sihon read the letting on the door. Kenneth Asquinn:

Chief Superintendent.

Bradan knocked on the door.

"Enter," and a voice within bid them. Bradan held the door open for Martha and Sihon to enter first, which he did with much reluctance. He had no desire to be interviewed by the police. He felt weak all over and his stomach churned. The office was large and well lit. There was glass half way down the corridor wall so the one inside the office could see what was going on in most other parts of the area at a glance.

Once inside the office Sihon found himself standing in front of a desk, and behind this desk sat Ken. A tingling feeling started at the nape of his neck and down to the tip of his fingers.

"Sit down," Ken invited the three of them.

Sihon sank into an ordinary steel structured but softly padded visitor's chair. Bradan sat in the chair next to him, Martha on Sihon's other side. The closeness made Sihon nervous. *What is the matter with me? He wondered. The presence of the police never made me nervous before.*

"Does he have to be here?" indicating Bradan. Sihon asked as if Bradan were no more than a bothersome gnat to be brushed from his shoulder.

"Yes, he does," Ken answered softly.

Martha handed Ken the envelope. "Sihon's Child Study Team records. Everything's there. His health records-everything you need to know."

"Thank you, Martha," Ken said, taking the offered documents, opened the folder and started to read. When he looked up his eyes rested on Sihon. He didn't speak for a long time.

Sihon squirmed in his chair. The office grew quiet. Sihon. Bradan and Martha waited for someone to say something.

Chapter Seven
Interviews

After reading the pages of Sihon's records in front of him for several minutes, Ken looked from Bradan to Martha seated across the desk from him, Sihon between them, then sighed loudly and said.

"You know Sihon, you're the only one in my long history of police work that has me baffled."

Ken looked at his sister and nodded.

Martha took this as a go ahead for her to start her questions with Sihon. "I don't even know where to begin with you anymore," Martha said. "You have never had difficulty relating to other people."

Sihon looked puzzled.

"What does that mean?" he asked in a disagreeable voice.

"You having difficulty relating to those that have been your friends for a long time. You have difficulty in talking to other people," Martha said gently. "It appears you don't know the first thing about establishing a relationship with someone your own age, anymore."

Martha's words surprised Sihon. How could she root out the problem so easily? But then maybe his lack of communication was only part of the problem, he thought.

"Why?" Martha asked.

"Why what?" Sihon said. Seated across the desk from him, Sihon between them

"Why don't you like people?" Ken repeated patiently.

The questions were asked in a soft, kind voice. This showed the man's skill in drawing teens out and talking about themselves. But Sihon wouldn't talk about his brief time away. He would never share his feelings with anyone. So he sat back in his chair and remained stubbornly silent.

After a few more minutes of this Ken sighed loudly once more and switched to another question. "How do you feel about yourself, Sihon?"

"I don't know." It reminded Ken of many years back when he was a kid, younger even than Sihon. He and Conrad Cameron, Sihon's uncle, were boys; and the exasperating conversations and arguments he had had with Sihon's uncle were much as he was having with his nephew right now.

"If you like yourself, others will," Bradan said carefully.

"What am I doing here?" Sihon said.

Tired of getting nowhere, Martha almost snapped "Where would you rather be?"

"Anywhere but in this police station. I don't have to tell you three anything about my stay at Cameron Estate. It's my life and I'll live it the way I like!"

"But you will remain here the entire hour and answer our questions," Ken said.

Sihon remained silent. He did not refuse to talk, but he struggled to put his words together to express himself in a way that would make sense. He was glad no one rushed him for answers.

"Take your time," Martha said instead.

After a moment of hard thinking, Sihon said, "I can't remember when I started disliking other kids. When I was little I looked forward to the day I would start school. I couldn't wait for that day to arrive."

Martha asked softly. "What changed?"

"'I don't know. They resent me. Conrad, Lillian, Mom, Dad, even Crystal. They were fine at first. Then Conrad found out he could not stop me from saying grace at the table or attending church with Mr. and Mrs. Willks, saying I missed devotionals in the evening, my Christian friends, and so on, they snickered at me. I know everyone in that household resented me."

"Why do they resent you?" Bradan asked.

"He told me he'd wanted a son to help with the business, likely to take over when he retired. Conrad, I'll call him by his name, he isn't my uncle, was very disappointed when their firstborn turned out to a girl and me not to be one bit interested in his multi million dollar business. I'd rather farm."

Sihon paused and bravely looked Ken in the eye, and continued. "I did everything in my power to get Dad to notice me."

"Is it important for him to like you?" Ken asked.

"It most certainly is. I wanted him to appreciate me. When nothing worked, I grew discouraged."

Sihon stopped talking. He couldn't speak; he fought back tears. Martha fetched some klenixes from her handbag and handed them to Sihon. Sihon dabbed his eyes with one, then shook himself.

"What's the matter with me? Why am I carrying on like this? Why do I feel so impatient with everyone I've loved for so long? It's like I'm two people."

Sihon sniffed. He felt like talking. He forgot that the man on the other side of the desk was an OPP Chief Superintendent and a second officer sat beside him. It made him feel good to get all his anxieties out in the open.

Ken said, "Conrad and his half-brother, Nigel, were sadly neglected by their parents as children. Conrad practically raised your Dad. Conrad controlled your Dad and a lot of other children through witch craft. A lot of kids in school were afraid of him."

"How did he control them?' Sihon asked.

Martha took up the story. "When Dad first came to The James Bay Frontier, witchcraft and evil spirits ruled her. Conrad, even though he was a mere six years old, was the high priest. Ever kid listened to him. Tell us more about your father, Sihon; familiarize us about his job."

"He doesn't work. He and Conrad own a gambling casino in Toronto. They also own a farm together that they use as their summer residence. Neither one farms the place himself."

"Did your father want to farm?" Bradan asked.

"I don't think so.

"Sihon, I'm going to try a system that I'm sure you will like," Martha said.

Sihon showed no interest; even his words seemed lifeless. "What's that, Nurse?"

Martha continued,"For any assignment Martin or Audrey, or any other adult for that matter, gives you, you will be paid $5.00; For not attending wild all night parties and going to bed early another $5.00: And For being polite and mannerly towards others, $2.00. How do you like it so far?"

Sihon's hazel eyes glowed bright for the first time since entering the office.

"Sounds wonderful!"

Martha continued. "But, money will be taken away from you every time you disobey these terms and are rude to people."

Thus emptied some of the eagerness from the boy.

Ken checked the hands on his wristwatch then leaned forward in his chair and said."The hour is drawing to a close, Sihon. Your next interview will be with Mrs. Martha Turehue, the public nurse."

Sihon suddenly felt afraid, remembering his rudeness towards her at their last meeting. "Why?"

Bradan said reassuringly. "She, like me and Ken, wish to locate the reason you act so hateful at times. You have been such a good-natured, happy boy up until now."

The next day after his interview with, on a hot afternoon, Sihon sat on the front steps listening to one of his rock tapes when he saw Wipinkino, Trever and Lorne on the road in front of the Martin's home, returning from checking the mail.

"Hi," Wipinkino said when the boys stopped where Sihon sat.

"Hi," Sihon answered politely, remembering his manners.

"It's a fine day," Trevor said.

"Any letters for me?" Sihon inquired.

Trevor leafed through the fat bundle of mail. He stopped and read the addresses then said.

"I don't believe there's a letter for you, Sihon."

Sihon followed his friends, and walked through the kitchen, and into the front room.

"I brought the mail in," Trevor said. He plopped the fat bundle down on the coffee table beside his Uncle Martin's chair. Kathleen read in a chair nearby.

"Thank you, nephew," Martin said

Sihon went to a couch and sat down, one leg folded underneath him. He was keenly disappointed, as he had expected to receive a letter from his Dad, Conrad, someone... Lorne walked over to the couch and sat down beside him. Trevor strolled over and took a seat on the other side of Sihon.

Sihon watched in amusement as Wipinkino walked over to Katkleen. Instead of sitting down close to her he knelt on his knees on the carpet by her chair.

Kathleen looked up from the pages of her book and smiled. Wipinkino flashed a brilliant smile back. "Care to come with me for some ice cream at van Ladisav's restaurant?"

Kathleen marked her place in the book and almost threw it aside in her eagerness.

"Sure, Wipinkino. Mom, Dad . . . she began but her parents had already witnessed her suitor's request.

"Yes go,Kathleen," Audrey urged.

"You can go," Martin said.

Wipinkino helped his date to her feet. Hand in hand they walked out of the room and outside. Sihon could see through the living-room window, they were still holding hands as they walked down the driveway then west on the road and appeared out of sigh.

That evening Sihon stepped out onto the back step. The full moon shone from a cloudless sky, making the night clear. A gentle, cool breeze freshened the muggy, heavy air of the day. He didn't notice Olvina or Phoebe at their bedroom window, looking out at the splendour of the moonlit world. Sihon didn't notice them watching as he ran down the driveway and turned towards downtown Forest Lake. It didn't occur to him that he wasn't supposed to be out this time of night. One 'clock in the morning? Way past curfew.

In the early morning hours a car rattled along the main drive of Forest Lake and stopped by Martin's driveway. Inside the car, Sihon climbed over two pairs of laps, to get out on the same side as the driver. He opened the door, slid and out.

"Good night," he said to those inside the car.

There was a chorus of "Good-night", but Sihon cut the voices off by slamming the car door shut. He sprinted for the back door which he'd sneaked out of only a few hours before . The moon had gone behind a dark cloud and rain sprinkled down, and a strong wind blew.

Sihon started towards the house, running the short distance and in through the door He tried not to slam the door, but a strong gust of wind and rain jerked the storm door from his hands. He tried not to cringe as the wind slammed the door on its hinges, up against the outside wall with a loud smack. Sihon crept through the kitchen, past the master bedroom door, through the front room and to his room. Finally, he pushed open the door of his bedroom. He undressed and fell into bed. He pulled the warm covers around him and soon fell asleep.

He didn't hear anyone enter his room later.

"Sihon, are you awake?"

"Yes."

The bed covers rustled as Sihon sat up. He peered up first at Olvina's head, then Cassia's.

"Did you just get in?"

"None of your business. Are you going to make an issue of it? Does any else know I sneaked out?"

"We do," Olvina said.

"Mom and Dad know," Cassia said.

"How did they find out? No one else was about when I went out or when I got back."

"Me and Phoebe saw you through our window," Olvina said. "We were sitting watching the moon."

"My sisters did what was best and told Mom and Dad," Cassia finished explaining.

"Great. I wish older sisters weren't invented. I'm not afraid. What can your Dad do?"

With those words Sihon pulled the covers over his head and was soon snoring.

Olvina and Phoebe looked at each other. They each rolled he eyes and shrugged. Soon they went back upstairs. Soon they, too, were also asleep.

The next morning, which was Saturday, Sihon slept late. When he did get up and dressed, Martin and Audrey were in the kitchen. There were no other kids around, and Martin wasted no time in getting down to the business at hand.

"Sit down," he told Sihon but the boy continued towards the door on his way outside. Sihon hesitated.

Martin repeated firmly. "Sit down."

Sihon didn't argue. He went to the table, pulled out a chair and sat down.

"I want to know what you were doing until five o'clock in the morning."

"It wasn't that late," lied Sihon. "I was home by midnight."

"Not according to Olvina and Phoebe. The girls came to us after midnight and told us you had sneaked out."

Sihon groaned silently within. With so many against him, what good would it do to lie?

He said brashly, "Okay so I sneaked out after midnight. So what? I was always out late at home. I never went to bed before dawn and I always slept in till noon."

"It never bothered your folks about what might happen to you?" questioned Audrey.

Sihon answered mutinously, "My Mom and Dad never worried. What could happen to me?"

"There's all kinds of danger," said Audrey.

"Nothing happened to me."

"I want to know what you did all night," Martin said.

"Nothing!"

"Nothing? You mean you wandered around Forest Lake all night, doing nothing?"

Sihon answered as if this behavior was the most natural in the world. "Yes."

"We have regulations in this household," Martin pointed out. "And if they're not obeyed, children are punished.

"I don't know what all the fuss is about," Sihon murmured mutinously.

"Five dollars will be taken away from your account," Sihon said.

Sihon said. "So what?"

Martin told the boy. "Continue this way until the end of the summer and you will end up with nothing or you can change your attitude and end up with merits to your credit. It's all up to you, Sihon. You can go now."

Sihon sprang to his feet.

"Where are you going?" inquired Martin.

"I'm going outside. I feel the need some fresh air."

"Be back in time for church," Audrey said.

"Yeah, yeah."

Sihon walked along the gravel allyway west towards where Ken lived. The youngest son, eleven-year-old Syd, rode his bicycle in the ally way road in behind of the house. Sihon stepped in front of him to stop him.

"What do you want?" Syd asked.

"I want your bike."

Syd tried to sound brave. "Well you can't have it."

"Oh is that so?' responded Sihon boldly. He grasped Syd by the shoulders and dragged him away from his bicycle then shoved him into the ditch along side the road. Sharp little stones bit into Syd's hands and knees as he fell.

"That's for those sisters ratting on me last night."

"What are you talking about?" Syd said as he struggled to his feet. He wiped dirt from his clothes. He looked at his hands. Blood ozzed from a cut at the end of one finger. He began to cry.

Hi Grace:

One of the things you should watch is having people talk and tell the reader about the action or conflict in the book, instead of showing it. So, for example, the two 'interviews' at the beginning of this chapter tell us that Sihon is being 'bad' but we don't really get to see him being bad, until very briefly at the end here when we actually see Sihon misbehaving for pretty much the first time, even though the adults are so upset about his behavior. Showing him steal the bike therefore brings the story to life for the reader, instead of just reading about people talking about his problems, etc.

Also, the interviews essentially say/do the same thing (with Ken and the Pastor even saying the same things). One might advance the plot but I'm not sure both do. With the Pastor, some new information is given about Conrad, which is good, and a plan is decided on which makes the stakes higher for Sihon – now if he misbehaves, he has to actually pay money, which is also good. In the interview with Ken, no new information is given, so the reader says to her/his-self, "I already know all this (from what's already been written); why should I keep reading?"

Novels are built out of scenes – and each scene advances the plot by making the circumstances more difficult for the main character and by building towards the climax – possibly that moment when Sihon does something really bad, almost unforgivable, and has to break out of Conrad's clutches or else be truly lost.

Let me know if you have any questions.

Chapter Eight
Sihon Meets New Friends

Four families had witnessed the incident right from the start.

Hearing the ruckus between Sihon and Syd, with Ken in the lead,he, Charlotte, and their sons, Brian and Raymond joined the crowd. .

Charlotte went to Syd and put a comforting arm around him. "Are you okay?"

Charlotte noticed the gash on the end of Syd's finger. She lifted the boy's hand for a better look. Blood gushed out the end of the finger and congealed in a red pool on the ground.

Bradan and Martha arived. Martha carried her black leather nurse's kit.

" Aunt Martha, my knee hurts," Syd said.

"May I?"

When Ken and Charlotte nodded, Martha knelt beside her young nephew and pulled up Syd's pantleg. Martha, Ken, and Charlotte gasped at two exposed gashed on his knee. Kneeling, Martha set the kit on the ground, opened the top and rummaged around inside. Her hand came out with a bottle of antiseptic and cotton batting. She set to work cleaning Syd's injuries.

Sihon spotted a young man quickly scaling the steep railroad embankment with ease. He leaped easily over each track and nimbly sprinted the distance and stopped in front of Gay-Anne and put an arm around her waist.

" Constable Barclay," Ken greeted the young officer.

"I heard shouting and noises coming from this direction, like two boys were having a scuffle."

"There certainly was," Ken answered. "Sihon pushed Syd off his bike and hurt him. artha is cleaning his wounds now. Thank you, Morley, about being concerned about my son."

" I wanted to help any way I can," the young man said.

Sihon had heard enough. After comforting their son, Sihon saw Ken and Charlotte approaching him. He picked up the fallen bike, leaped on it and rode away.

Syd shouted after him. "Hey, give me back my bike."

Sihon kept on peddling.

"That's my bike! Sihon that's my bike. I hate you! I hate you!"

Ken reached out and took the boy's hand in his. "We'll get it back, son.

Ken next approached Martin and Audrey, still holding Syd's hand. His face was unforgiving as he spoke to the couple, "Martin, Audrey, that boy of yours is getting out of control. Get him in check or he goes back to his parents."

"We will, Ken," Audrey promised.

"We will," Martin assured his brother.

That same evening at seven o'clock, the biggest part of the members of the little church gathered for services, But Sihon was conspicuously absent.

Sihon continued out of town on Syd's three speed bicycle. He'd reached the big north, south, highway and was moving along for all he was worth. He wanted to peddle and peddle and never stop. He'd come to the North Blanche River Bridge when a carload of teen-agers stopped beside him. It was the gang from the beach party.

"There you are, Sihon."

"Hi, Vanna," replied Sihon.

"Why are you riding around on that cumbersome bike? Come with us and we'll give you a real ride in this beauty," Vanna said. "Get rid of that bicycle. Just toss it into the river. No one will find it there." .

Sihon hoisted the bicycle above his head and hurled it into the murky water. It landed in the water with a swoosh, then plunged downward with a twist and sank out of sight amidst the silt and dirt on the bottom.

Sihon dashed for the car where Vanna held the door open for him as if he were now a hero. Sihon slid into the back seat beside her. Sihon knew them all. Kirby Weston drove. Sihon knew Kirby Weston's preence in Forest Lake went back as far as Tadcu and Mamcu's, and the family. Kirby's grandfather, Terry Weston, had died in a fire Conrad and his devil worshiping followers, had intended Ken to die in. But the so called curse on Ken backfired. Accidentally, upon returning home that cold and stormy night, Terry overheated the wood furnace by putting on too much wood. The furnace over heated and the following fire destroyed the Weston's house. Terry, Kirby's grandfather, died in the fire. Terry's parents, and also a youner brother, which was Kirby's father, also named Kirby, survived. No, there was no love for the Asquinn family found in families of the Westons. Kirby's girl, Cora sat beside him while Vanna and Sihon sat in the back seat. Kirby was three years older than Sihon.

Sihon suddenly felt nervous. The inside of the car seemed to shrink, he found it difficult to breath. He wanted out, he even reached for the car door handle, but Kirby had the car moving now.

"Home is boring and I'm looking for some excitement." Sihon said. "They expect me to be back in time for church at seven o'clock. What squares!"

"How old are you?" Cora said.

"Old enough," said Sihon.

A look passed between Vanna and Kirby.

Kirby said to Sihon. "You've come to the right place. Just hang on. We found ourselves a real speedster this evening to have fun with. Me, Vanna and Cora stole it right out of someone's driveway. The police will never be able to catch us."

Sihon knew Kirby was a high school drop out. With a lot of time on his hand he was in a lot of trouble continuously with the police.

That same night, while Sihon was out joyriding, at Turehue's, Gerald sat to one side of his father and Morley in the kitchen. Gerald was a mirror of his father. He had the same dark hair, brown eyes and the enjoyment of life bubbling from him.

Both the officers were in uniform as they were on call during the graveyard shift. Outside the world give the impression of being still and dark as it was way past midnight. The kitchen blazed with light from overhead bulbs.

Bradan said to Gerald, his oldest son, "Quit your job as anchorman on the six o clock news show on CTLH? "

"That's right, Dad," Gerald said. "I want to be a policeman like you and Uncle Ken. Like my brother, Lyle, and cousin Kirk. Those two are all set to start police training in the fall."

"What brought about this sudden decision?"

"It wasn't sudden," explained Gerald. "Ever since I 've worked as tv journalist, I've decided I don't like the job. After praying about this all summer, that's what I know God wants me to do with my life."

Bradan was too surprised to come up with any immediate response. Gerald asked. "Don't you like the idea?"

"Oh sure I do. I'm proud of you both and your mother and I support you all the way. When were you planning on attending Police College?"

Gerald said, "Do you think it would be possible for Uncle Ken to help out here? I'd like to start in September if that's possible."

"It would be a good idea to talk to your Uncle Ken about it."

"I've quit my job as sports reporter for TV," were Gerald's next words.

Bradan reminded his firstborn, "Ger, you're a married man. How do you expect to support yourself and Joan and your sons, Philip and Darryl?"

"I was hoping you would help Joan and me out there, Dad. I would like to remain unemployed for the rest of the summer to enjoy the few weeks of freedom I have left."

"You mean live here with your wife and sons until school starts?"

"That's what I mean. Please Dad. You don't know what it's like to work at a job that your heart isn't in."

"Oh, I think I do. Your Uncle Ken and I left home when we were younger than you. We thought there was better somewhere else. In a short time we regretted this action with bitter tears and came back home to family and church. My heart goes out to you, son. I want to do what I can to help you get that job of your heart. All right we'll talk to your Uncle Ken about college this fall and see what he has to say."

"Thanks Dad," Gerald said.

Lyle, the second oldest, descended the stairs and joined the two policemen and Gerald. He was three years younger than Gerald, with lilic coloured eyes.

"What are you doing up at this hour?" Bradan demanded.

"I just heard over the late, late news about a car being stolen right from the owner's driveway," Lyle said. "There's some teen-agers making a lot of noise out by the South Blance River. I heard Sihon's name. He's with this wild bunch."

Just then the telephone rang. Morley quickly picked up the receiver then handed it over to Bradan.

"Your brother-in-law, Martin," he said.

***

Ken sat in a comfortable recliner in his front room. The glow from a lamp sitting on an end table surrounded him, but the rest of the room was dark. He set some sheaves of paper he'd been studying, material he would have to know to make informed decisions for the coming day at work, and leaned back resting his head on the back of the chair and closed his eyes.

His eldest son came down the stairs and joined him.

"Dad, do you have a second?" inquired Murray. With sandy coloured hair, blue eyes and good looks, Murray was an exact image of his father at twenty-one.

"I always have time to listen to others, Murray. I thought you would be in bed, sleeping at three in the morning."

"I couldn't sleep."

"Come on out and tell me. What's bothering you?"

"Dad," Murray began. "You must know I've never been happy in this job as anchor news broadcaster for TV; I feel so inadequate because my heart isn't in it. I've already quit my present job."

Ken was amazed. "Quit your job, and you a married man

and with a family on the way? What would you rather be doing, son?"

"I've prayed a lot asking God's guidance in what He would have me pick as a career."

"And you know that whatever you choose, if it's within reason that is, both your mother and I will stand by you

"And I appreciate that. I appreciate the job I have while I sorted out my life. My cousin Ger seems to have everything together. He's married and has started his own family. Now I think I've sorted out my life. I know what I want to do this fall. I'm hoping you will help me out with this."

"I want to hear what you've decided before I make any promises," his father said.

"I want to be an Ontario Provincial Police officer. I'm hoping you would help me."

"And how could I help you? What about yours and Tamara's plans?"

"Tammy and I have talked this over, and she says she's willing to go along with whatever God would have me do."

"Oh she is? I'll talk to her later today and see for myself how she feels about all this."

"Maybe I could work for the department for the rest of the summer so I could get a feel for the job and determine whether that's what I really want."

"That can be arranged. Instead of only one son attending police college in the fall, there will be two," Ken said.

"Thanks, Dad," Murray said graciously.

"You're welcome son," his father said pleasantly.

"And could I work with the department here in Forest Lake?"

"You most certainly can" Ken said.

Just then two-way radiophone on an end table by Ken's chair warbled. Ken said to his sons. "Excuse me. That's likely Uncle Bradan. I wonder why he's calling me at this hour?"

Ken pressed the call button and spoke. "Yes, Bradan."

"Good morning to you too, Ken," came Bradan's jovial response. "How did you know it was me calling?"

"Just a guess," replied the chief superintendent. "Anyway, you're the only one that calls me on this phone so late. What's up that's so important?"

"I just received a call from Martin, your brother."

This caught Ken's attention instantly. "Oh? What's wrong in that household?"

"Apparently Sihon's been out all night again. Martin said the kid went out just before dark and he hasn't been seen since."

"What do you expect me to do about it?" Ken asked lightly.

"I phoned to find out what you wanted to do. Would you want to accompany Constable Barclay and me on this call or would you rather just the two of us went? I realize you don't often work anything but days."

"I never work anything but days, Sergeant," Ken corrected him.

"But you've said more than once to let you know when your brother calls headquarters. And you did say night or day."

"I know I have Bradan, and I appreciate you calling," Ken said then paused. He pulled back one corner of the drapes and looked out into the dark night. A warm, friendly, yellow, glow radiated from the street and yard floodlights but what lurked beyond in the darkness, he didn't know.

"I've also received a report about a car being stolen from a man's yard and a bunch of teen agers partying in a field out by North Blanch River Road," Bradan said. "The stolen car was a courtesy car."

It took Ken several minutes to decide what to do. "All right, I'll go with you. Where are you now? You must be on graveyard shift?"

"I'm calling from home. I'm on call this week, so is Barclay. He's here too."

"I'll be ready when you and Constable Barclay get here," Ken said and ended the call.

"Going out on a call, Dad?" Murray asked.

"Yes,"

An idea struck Murray. "Can I come along? I'll stay out of the way, I promise. I won't be any trouble."

"Come on, Uncle Bradan and Constable Barclay are here already."

Chief Superintendent Asquinn and his son stepped out into the damp chilly night and walked to the cruiser and slid into the back seat.

Ken said pleasantly, "Good morning Seargant Turehue, Constable Barclay. Constable, meet my oldest son, Murray. Murray, Barclay's been with the department only three weeks."

"Good morning Ken, Murray," replied Bradan.

"Good morning," responded the Constable.

If either was surprised to see Murray accompanying his father, neither said anything. Constable Barclay drove and had the car underway as soon as the doors closed.

"You can rest assured that I'm doing this only for my brother," Ken said. Bradan looked back at his brother-in-law and grinned. "I don't believe that for a moment. I realize you don't appreciate being called out at this unfriendly hour of the morning, but you don't have to keep reminding me. You've agreed to this at three o'clock in the morning because you care about Sihon as well as your brother." "

"Phooey," responded Ken.

"I've never known you to be callused, Ken," Bradan said.

"All right, have it your way Bradan if that's what you think," Ken said, allowing radan to win this little tiff in fun.

This didn't make Bradan feel good at all. He glanced at Morley and then Murray and Ken last. He felt they were all having a good chuckle at his expense.

"There's more. Martin came and got Charlotte and me earlier. Sihon knocked my youngest son off his bike and took it away from him."

Constable Barclay blushed as Bradan teased.

"And I might add, Morley, here, walked with Gay."

Ken said in jest, "And then took her out to church this evening; I know, I was at church." Then said more seriously. "That kid is getting meaner and meaner."

"And there was a convertible stolen from where it was parked in a driveway in front of the garage," Bradan said. "The stolen car was reported before the partying teens."

"Did the caller say how many in the group?" questioned Ken.

"He thinks five," replied Bradan then said to Constable Barclay. "Hang a right here, Constable and half in a mile hang a left."

Sihon and his companions were all seated in the car.

Vanna shivered and snuggled closer to Sihon. In the back seat Cora and Kirby snuggled closer. A liquor bottle passed from hand to hand. When it came to Sihon, he grabbed the object and holding it to his lips, took a long drag.

Vanna intervenned, "Here let me have that."

She took the bottle from him, drew a little from it and passed it back to Cora.

"The night has cooled as the sun has set,and the mosquitoes are bad" Sihon said. "

Someone please put the top up." His words were slurred already.

"Are you having a good time yet, Sihon?" Vanna asked.

"I sure am."

""So am I."

"And me."

"Me, too."

"Count me."

The night was black when Kirby opened the door. "I have to get a breath of fresh air," he said.

The rest stayed in the car. The driver's seat remained empty. Sihon looked and looked at the empty space and tried to tell himself that only a fool would do what ran through his mind. But whatever got inside him caused him to open the back door and move to the driver's seat then shut and lock the door behind him.

It didn't take Kirby long to get back to the car. "What are you doing?"

"I'm going to drive. You've been driving all evening."

Kirby didn't argue and slid into the back seat beside Cora.

"Maybe we should move to another spot," Sihon said.

"Those 'church quads' uncles will likely drive by here any minute," Cora hiccuped.

"Who are 'the church quads?" inquired Sihon.

"Don't you know?" asked Vanna. "They're Olvina, Phoebe, Kathleen, Cassia and Eunice."

"That family really thinks they're better than the rest of us," Kirby said.

"And just because one is the Chief Superintendent," Cora put in her two cents worth.

"A car's coming," Kirby said. "It could be the cops.

"It is," Vanna said. "I hear the siren."

Sihont froze, not knowing what to do next.

"Well come on, man, you said you could drive. Get going!" ordered Kirby.

Sihon switched on the engine and with much spinning of tires, spun the car around and shot out of the space they'd parked in, missing the police car by a mere millimeter.

"Way to go, Sihon!" whooped Vanna.

The car's headlights caught the cruiser in its glow for a short period of time, as was the car Sihon drove caught in the glow of the cruiser's headlights.

"It's them," said Vanna. "I recognized Sergeant Turehue and the one they call Constable Barclay."

"But I saw others in the back seat," Sihon said. "I'll keep ahead and make sure they don't catch us."

In the cruiser Bradan asked. "Ken, did I see right or was that really Sihon driving that car?"

"You saw right," Ken said.

"He doesn't look old enough to be driving even with a licensed driver beside him," Constable Barclay said.

"He isn't," Ken said.

The Chief Superintendent's lips tightened. "That kid's digging himself further and further into trouble."

Back in the stolen car, Vanna instructed Sihon. "Now all you have to do is stay ahead of them."

But Sihon didn't need telling. After turning north onto the main highway, he pressed his foot down on the accelerator and the car shot forward like a rocket.

"The cops have turned around now," Vanna said.

"They still have to get onto the main highway," Sihon said.

"And then they'll be after us," giggled Vanna.

"We'll be miles ahead," Sihon said joyfully.

Sihon didn't release the pressure on the gas pedal. The powerful car responded to his slightest touch. As they passed houses along the way, he noticed all buildings were in darkness. Most people slept at this hour; But not him, for once he was out in the night having fun.

Sihon turned his head and looked out the back window. "The cops aren't even in sight.

"Sihon, hang a left by that gravel road," Vanna said.

But the instructions came too late. Sihon saw the side road Kirby had told him about and wanted to follow instructions and turn onto it, but his mind had too much to think about, and clouded with liquor, made him miscalculate and fail to turn. With screeching and smoking tires the car swerved and missed the turn all together. There was a really steep bank at the shoulder of the highway and rocks at the bottom of the gulch. The carload of teens plunged over this embankment. Vanna and Cora screamed. Kirby shrieked. "Sihon!"

Sihon covered his face with his arms and moaned, "Oh no! I'm in trouble now!"

There was much clamor and screaming, as the car sailed through the air, then seemed to remain suspended for an eternity before it took a sharp nosedive down. From far below came the sound of crumpling metal and breaking glass as the car came to a sudden, lurching stop on top of the rocks. And then silence. No one moved. Sihon lay in a heap on the rocks.

Sihon moaned. His eyes opened. He shook his head, raised himself to his elbow and through a haze, started wrestling the driver's door , wriggled out just in time to see Cora and Kyle sneaking away from the crash site. Vanna remained in the car but didn't move. Cora hurried to join Kirby.

Out on the highway Sihon heard the police siren wail. The cruiser soon came into sight and slowed for the turn.

"Hurry," Sihon said. "I must get out of here. No cop is going to find me.Those snoopy cops won't find us here. I'm too smart for them. That puffed up Superintendent with his inflated ego won't get the better of me. I know a place to hide until the cops go away," Sihon said. Looking back down the hill, he could plainly see the wreck site and hear moans of pain from Vanna and cries for help. Vanna groaned and struggled to rise to her feet.

"Help me."

Sihon covered his ears with a hand in a effort to block out the painfilled groans and cries for help.

"Help me, please," Vanna begged.

Sihon started back towards the wreck.

Kyle or Cora didn't even hesitate, or reach out a hand to assist.

Together the two of them half fell and half ran further down the slope in order to escape.

The police cruiser arrived with lights flashing and siren blaring. Sihon put his hands over his ears to shut out the noise. The instant the driver parked the car Ken was out and in action. "Bradan, you check the car and I'll call an ambulance. Constable, you go with him. You too,

Murray."

Murray and Constable Barclay followed Bradan down the steep embankment to the car far below. This particular spot was still in the shade, therefore the interior of the car lay in darkness. Constable Barclay switched on his powerful flashlight and shone the beams through the crumpled glass in the windows.

"What do you see, Constable?" inquired Bradan.

"One teen trapped between the seat and the door," replied the Constable. Just then Ken joined them.

"The ambulance is on its way," he told his co-workers. He too used his flashlight to seek out clues inside the car.

Murray gagged. "Wow, what a smell. I've never experimented with liquor."

Sihon stopped beside Ken. Murray turned to Sihon, "I have a feeling young kids like these four should not have been drinking stuff like this." He quickly ran for some bushes and promptly threw up.

"The ambulance is here," Bradan said as the vehicle, with siren wailing, drew up along side the cruiser.

"We'll come back to this later," Ken said. "Murray don't walk around the area surrounding the car until we've had more time to search out clues."

Sihon watched in silence as the ambulance workers separated a very still and pale teen from the wreck and loaded in the ambulance.

"You come with us," one of the paramedics told Sihon, "You banged your head terribly. There's a bruise forming on your forehead, already."

The second paramedic helped Sihon into the ambulance and the two teens were whisked away to the Lakeview hospital.

"They'll soon be gone," Kirby said to Cora, thinking the cruiser would follow the ambulance, but the three policemen and Murray returned to searching for clues.

"Darn," Kirby said.

Together Ken and his men looked for clues available in the wet sand and grass immediately outside the car, then beyond.

"Look at this," Bradan said. "Boot tracks and they aren't adult and they lead further down that embankment."

"Then there were more than two in the car," Constable Barclay said.

Ken agreed. "That's right. There are two sets of tracks."

"I know Dad, there were four teens in the car and two got away," Murray burst out.

"Thank you for your answer. But you agreed to not get in the way, remember?"

"There were four but two didn't get away," Constable Barclay said, then added. "They are merely hiding amongst those rocks down there."

"I agree with you," Ken said.

"Do you want Constable Barclay and me to go down there?" inquired Bradan. "It wouldn't take us long to root them out."

Bradan's brown eyes swept over the terrain surrounding them. Muskeg stretched for miles behind that pile of rocks, and nothing but rocky cliffs and deep valleys following the road.

"Those kids don't realize it, but there's no place to go but back into the arms of the police,"

"No need for that, Bradan." Ken stood up and Bradan, Constable Barclay, and Murray did the same.

"We might as well move along," Bradan said loud enough for his voice to carry in the still, crisp air to the hiding youths. "It looks like they've given us the slip."

"They're coming," Ken said. Four black ravens appeared in the sky flying from wherever ravens spend the night to what ever they do during the day. Suddenly one left his companions, squawked and dove at something out of sight of the officers. "Those ravens told on them."

But still the officers didn't make any kind of move.

"You wait here Murray and stay here until I say it's okay."

Soon two heads appeared above the rim of the canyon. The sun was well above the treetops now and would soon beat down on the earth below creating unbearable heat, but drying out the slippery rocks, grass and underbrush. All was silent. The upper part of the bodies appeared, and then they were on level ground. "See, nobody's here," Kirby crowed. He had no way of knowing Murray waited with the three policemen. His voice boomed and resounded in the quiet and crisp air and carried right to the ears of the waiting officers. "I told you I was smarter than that high and mighty Superintendent."

Then all cockiness drained from Kirby like sails going limp in a sudden lull in the wind when he saw Ken and his two officers step out silently from behind the pile of blasted rocks. Kirby looked behind him. *Ken must have waited until the boys had walked several yards away from the rim of the canyon then softly instructed his men that now was the time, Kirby thought.*

"You wait here, Murray," his Dad told him.

Constable Barclay blocked the way to the highway so the car thieves couldn't escape this way while Bradan stepped behind them so the youngsters couldn't flee back down the way they'd come.

"Good morning," Ken said.

With a sigh of exasperation and defeat, Kirby and Cora seemed to deflate of all arrogance and pride.

"Arrest them and read them their rights," Ken ordered Constable Barclay.

"I believe we've just apprehended the two that stole the car that was wrecked here," said.

Kirby challenged, defiant to the end. "What makes you think I stole it? Sihon was driving so it was him that stole the car."

Kirby added to the story when no one else spoke, "He's right. Cora and me were just walking along the road when Sihon pulls up in this car and invites us all out for a joyride. He was out there driving wild ,like, all night."

Ken said. "We'll see. Vanna and Sihon were taken to the hospital immediately. He has a terrible lump on your forehead, right along the hairline."

Bradan opened the one back door and helped Cora to be seated. On the other side, Murray helped Morley assist Kirby into the back seat.

That afternoon Vanna was visiting Sihon. She hadn't been discharged yet and wore her hospital gown and slippers. She stood by Sihon's hospital bed when the girls entered the room. "How do you feel?" Olvina asked.

Sihon replied bravely, "Okay. My head doesn't hurt anymore. Not much anyway." Fear suddenly churned in Sihon's stomach. "I'm going to be all right, aren't I? Is Vanna all right?"

"The Doctor says both of you will be all right," Cassia said.

"Your head will hurt for weeks after that junk you four kids drank,"

Kathleen assured the younger boy.

Sihon merely groaned.

"Sihon, who stole that car?" Phoebe asked.

Sihon remained silent, looking from one face to the other, trying to read their thoughts but the faces were expressionless.

"I guess I'm sorta to blame for this. "Your Dad warned me to stay away from kids like Kirby."

But he wasn't about to admit to drinking or using any kind of drugs, he thought.

"You're not going to tell us who stole that car?" Cassia said.

Sihon objected. "Why should I? I'm not saying nothing. I'm not going to inform on my friends."

the girls exchanged disgusted looks.

"Sihon, those four are putting all the blame on you Vanna said. "They're saying you stole the vehicle, and picked them up for a joy ride."

"We may as well go," Eunice said, "we're not getting any cooperation from him. A typical ending to a wild night out."

"I'm glad you can joke about it," Phoebe said, tight-lipped.

"Oh sure, why not develop a sense of humor."

"Because if Sihon continues to refuse to tell who the real thieves are he's throwing away his entire future," Phoebe said. "That's the way it is in Ontario, if a young person steals a vehicle, he's throwing away his entire future."

"We have to go," Eunice told the younger boy.

"But you just got here. How did you get into Lakeview from Forest Lake?"

"We came in by public transport on the bus," Olvina said. "We'll see you, Sihon."

Tuesday evening Sihon sat across the desk in Aunt Martha's office. His eyes took on a distant look and he folded his hands together, rested his elbows on his knees, and his head on his hands. The two were alone.

"I believe my brother was questioning you when we were interrupted," Martha said. "I want to continue along those lines."

Martha paused, drew a deep breath and plunged into the task at hand. "What did you do for two hours after getting off the train?"

"I guess I had some pretty wild thoughts. I was so discouraged because I thought no one cared for me that I tried to slash my wrists."

" Now we're starting to get somewhere," Martha said. "No one was there to meet you because we weren't told you were coming."

Sihon replied politely.

"I realize that now."

Martha reached out and grasped Sihon'ss hand and examined his wrists. "You actually started to, didn't you?"

Sihon nodded.

"What stopped you?"

Sihon remained silent. Martha drew an impatient breath, wondering if he refused to cooperate again.

"Did someone show up and interrupt?" she said patiently.

When Sihon refused to answer, Martha said patiently, "Answer my questions, please."

"I'm not sure that I can answer that, Ma'am," Sihon said respectively. "I don't know what stopped me, all I know is I'd already started the incision and suddenly I had an urgent drive to reach Martin's. That happened twice, once while I was still at the station waiting and the other when I stopped to rest on my walk to the house and oh yes, once more right by their back door. I don't understand it but some force was protecting me yesterday morning."

"You should. God and His holy angels are not foreign to you.'

Sihon's reply came from the heart. "But I want to understand. Why doesn't somebody explain it all to me instead of hating me?"

"We don't hate you, Sihon," Martha said kindly. "Neither do we tolerate insolence from children your age. It's Mr. Cameron that hates you, not us. And you will be taught about what God now that you're with Martin and family. I can guarantee that."

"That all sounds good to my ears."

"Sihon, you had every opportunity for assistance in reaching Martin's place when you arrived. The conductor even told you to go across the street to the police station and your answer was quote "Naw". I'd rather spend the night alone than ask a policeman to help me." unquote."

Sihon had the decency to feel his face burn in embarrassment. "I've since deeply regretted not taking the conductor's advice."

Martha showed his doubts when a chuckle escaped her lips. "We'll see how long that regret stays with you. Continue."

"My cousin, Crystal, Conrad's daughter, and I were never encouraged to trust or even talk to policemen. On my side of the family cops are regarded as the enemy. Conrad was continually cursing them because they're always raiding their Casinos; they even shut them down several times. But they always managed to open again. Conrad telling us to never trust a policeman and his running them down all the time must have gotten embedded in me somehow."

Martha made no comment on this, but she did ask, "What are you doing up here in the first place? You were sent back home only three weeks ago, for the summer. There's five weeks before school starts."

Sihon confessed. "Conrad and I had----words. He's disowned me, rather, I disowned him and he's disinherited me. When I was put on the north bound train I thought they'd already notified someone here that I was coming."

Martha looked straight at Sihon. "No more questions for now. There's much more to be considered than they cared to indulge into this evening. However, I did wish to let you know there will be more meetings and investigating and decisions made. And Conrad or your father will have to be brought into court for treating you like this. That's negligence. Leaving a thirteen-year-old boy alone for twelve hours at an enormous, bustling casino. Something tragic could have happened to you. Crystal might be taken away from him."

"I fear for Crystal. Maybe she will come to live with Martin and Audrey, permanently," Sihon said. A sunlit smile spread across his face. Martha also smiled. Sihon seemed to talk to her instead of around her or through her or as if she wasn't even there. For the first time in a long while, Sihon actually smiled.

"You will continue these sessions. You missed more than you attended before."

"I don't mind," Sihon said quickly.

Martha paused then she went onto another subject. "Is there anything else is on your mind that's important?"

"I didn't steal that car. I'm tired of holding back and covering up for the real thieves."

"And who are the real thieves?" Martha asked.

Sihon said without hesitation, "Kirby and Cora. Vanna was already with then by the time I got into the car. Kirby even boasted about it while we were driving around. I'm glad to get this mess out into the open. There were four of us in the car. Kirby, Cora and me took off but I returned when I realized Vanna was trapped and hurt. I realize Kirby intends for me to take the blame."

"The police already know about the other two. They arrested them on the scene the very same day. They aren't sure who actually stole the car. They, of course, said you did," Martha said

Sihon said brightly, "Vanna told me she would back up my story."

More doubtful looks passed across Martha's face. " Ken promised he'll have Uncle Bradan talk to all the kids involved that night, and check your story out. If you're telling the truth he might be able to get some of the charges against you dropped."

"And I will have my future back, and I, will have a real home, again." Sihon said. He breathed freely for the first time since he could remember. He felt a warm feeling spread through him. It was the first time he felt any kind of emotion calling anyplace home. He stood up to leave.

"Sihon, before you go, I'll say this," Martha said,. 'Between now and our next meeting, think back over your visit with Conrad."

"I'd rather forget it," Sihon said.

"This is important," Martha assured him. "Think about what you saw. What did he say to you? Why do you think Crystal is in danger? Did you see him mistreating her. Think back and bring back to me all that you recall."

"I will, Ma'am"Sihon promised.

Chapter Nine
Freed From Guilt

On Sihon's return home, Wapinkino finished mowing and raking Martin's lawn. Olvina and Phoebe waited on the top front step, while Cassia, Kathleen and Eunice perched on the steps below. Trevor leaned against the wall nearby.

The front door opened and Audrey appeared. She held some money in her hand.

'Here you are, Wapinkino, payment for cleaning up the yard. I know your family can use the money for food. Mrs. Olson doesn't receive much in support since Mr. Olson left."

"Thank you, Mrs. Asquinn," Wapinkino said as he took the bills. Audrey turned and went back into the house.

"How did your meeting with Aunt Martha go?" Olvina asked Sihon.

"Better than I ever imagined. Much better than the first meetings."

"Glad to hear that," Trevor said.

"Doesn't cooperating once in awhile make you feel better?" Phoebe said.

Sihon came away from the meeting with the public health nurse feeling good about himself. The last doubts about himself and his low self-esteem melted away.

"Let's go swimming now," he said.

"Where's Owen?" inquired Sihon. "We never see much of him."

"Owen has a job and he works Saturdays, evenings included," Olvina said. "We likely won't see him until after nine o'clock or maybe even not until church on Sunday."

Olvina stood up and said to he sister, "Let's go see if Mom needs any help."

She went into the house using the same door her mother had. Her four sisters stood and followed.

" I will have to go home, first," Wapinkino said.

"I'll go with you," Sihon said.

"I'll wait for by the railroad crossing," Trevor volunteered.

Sihon followed wapinikono at a run along the trail to his house. The trail passed through some think woods for a short distance. A small boggy creek ran through the woods to empty into Lake Forest only a few yards away. In the spring, run off from melting ice on the lake swelled the stream considerably. The stream was still high from spring melt. Small Willow trees and poplar trees had been cut from the forest, and a rickety pole bridge built to span the bog.

The thick and dreary forest where the branches were so dense the sun did not get through, made Sihon suddenly think of Conrad's place. The darkness, the mansion that reminded him of a haunted house, the evil surrounding the tall mansion and grounds and oozed from every corner of the interior.

As silent as swift as the Snow Owl, which was Wapinkino's native name, he ran with little effort.

At last the boys came out of the woods to a clearing where there were two summer cottages. Both were occupied. Both well kept up and well maintained. The boys had to pass these cottages in order to reach Wapinkino's house way at the end of the line. Sihon couldn't but help notice the path being overgrown with an entanglement of weeds and thistles. The house was shabby, the windows cracked and dirty. The roof missed a lot of it's shingles, the siding torn off by the wind, more than likely, Sihon thought, from the sides of the hose. Five children, ranging in ages from toddler to twelve, played in the dirt outside.

"Hello, Aris," Sihon spoke to one boy, the second oldest of twelve. He knew most the Olson children from school. Aris would be in grade eight in the fall. Then a girl, Nadine. Another boy named Bobby, nine years old, six-year old Susan and three year old Eileen. *Crystal and Nadine* would be the same age. Funny, Sihon thought, why should he think of Crystal at that moment? It didn't end there. His mind went back to how Conrad; not just Conrad, but Crystal's mother, Sihon's mother and father spoke to the girl. All were snippish and curt with her, Conrad was especially gruff. Sihon remembered Martha asking him to think back about how these four could be abusing Crystal. Sihon was certain now that this was one way to abuse a child- verbally.

Wapinkino entered the house through the back door which led right into the kitchen. It shocked Sihon to see the middle of the kitchen floor had caved in.

Sihon found his friend in a cluttered living-room talking to Mrs. Olson. Sihon noticed she was mostly Native.

"Mrs. Asquinn gave me money today for cleaning up their yard, Mom," Wapinkino said. "I want you to have it."

"Thank you ," Mrs. Olson said. "I will go to Weston's General store later and buy some food."

"Can I go swimming now,Mom?" Wapinkino asked.

"Go ahead," his mother answered.

Sihon preceded Wapinkino outside. Sihon waved at the younger children as the boys started back over the trail they'd just traveled. The children waved back and called out their good-byes.

The boys came to the slim tree trunk bridge again. Wapinkino crossed, then Sihon started across. From this direction, the bog looked deeper. Sihon's thoughts took wings and he thought of Conrad's place again. He had been so engrossed with his thoughts, he lost his balance.

"Oh," he shouted as he tottered on one of the thin poles. Sihon tottered some more, he waved his arms for balance.

"Auuuuug, help me. Wapinkino!"

Wapinkino appeared. "Oh, my. I thought you were capable of crossing this so-called bridge."

"I 'm losing my concentration and I'll fall" Sihon said. "Help me."

The Indian youth had to wade into the bog in order to grasp his friend's hand. He then guided Sihon across the makeshift bridge to boggy ground, then the more solid trail.

Sihon and Wapinkino joined Trevor at the railroad crossing.

Sihon walked between Wapinkino and Trevor down to the beach.

"What were you think about?" Trevor asked ."How come you almost lost your balance and fall into the bog?'

"I was thinking about witchcraft and evil spirits."

"Why them?" Wapinkino asked. "Evil possess people, and cause nothing but harm to people the possessed person wants harmed."

'You can learn all about demons in the encyclopedia," Trevor said.

"Thanks, guys," Sihon said. "I'll do that."

After that, Sihon was silent on the walk down to the public beach. His silence was not an angry silence, as it would have been earlier in the summer. Trevor and Wapinkino had sensed his state of mind, and knowing he needed some sort of assurance and comfort, spoke to him kindly. Earlier others had listened to his grievances; No other persons had shown him such consideration.

Sihon woke up late one night. His bedroom was on the ground level of the house, facing north. The second bedroom off the kitchen, and faced east belonged to Martin and Audrey.

Sihon's room was pitch dark. He didn't understand why. Usually enough light from outside, the moon or stars, came in through the window to light the room. He didn't understand why until he saw a flash of lightning and follwed by a crash of thunder. A storm approached.

This brought about thoughts of Conrad's house. He remembered the roofs with their iron wrought decorations, the arched windows, and the tower dominating the entire structure. The words, *witchcraft, voodoo,* and black magic kept running through his mind. He tosses and turned. He knew very little about what any of the words implied. He didn't know anything about voodoo dolls, but as the storm outside was upon him, his thoughts grew more and more chaotic and jumbled. Lightning crashed outside and thunder rumbled extra loud.

Sihon threw back his covers and up in a flash. Taking the flashlight he always kept handy inside his bedside dresser, In his pyjamas, he made his way to his bedroom door, opened it, looked out and peeked around. No one else up. He walked as silently as he could across the kitchen floor to the living-room doorway. He didn't remember there being so many squeaks in the kitchen floor before. He paused and looked to the bookcases filled with books. A lot of the books were for him and the girls' ages, but some younger, or older. He knew the household boasted of a set of *Encyclopedia Britannica*.

He continued his stealth to the bookcase he remembered the set of red leather bound books were stored. He'd even used then before for research work in school assignments. He ran his gaze along the spines of the alphabetically order shelved books and took from the shelf two he felt he wanted.

Without turning on the lights, he then carried the two heavy books to the couch where he set them on the coffee table.

He opened one book at the very start and, by flashlight, started to read. All was quiet within the house and outside as he read. Noise of the storm appeared to have subsided, then there was a particularly brilliant flash of lightning. Yellow light lit up the living room. Thunder rumbled outside, not once but twice.

"Oh," Sihon cried as one bolt of lightning hit close to the house.

He continued to read.

At last Sihon closed all three books. He looked out the window. "So that's how you control people. It's not going to work .I have God on my side. He's more powerful than any demon."

Sihon closed his books and without replacing them, crept back to his bed. Smiling and at peace, he fell asleep immediately. The storm blowing outside didn't bother him. Once during the night he woke to find the storm had blown itself out. All was calm. He smiled and went back to sleep.

And as a result of his talk with the Martha, Sihon sat across the desk from her the following Monday. She came around to the front of her desk and sat on one corner. She towered above Sihon who sat tall and straight in his chair. For once closeness didn't intimidate him, in fact this sort of alliance made him feel good. He could feel warmth and communication flowing between him and Martha.

"We'll go back to the fight between you and Conrad," Martha said.

"What about it? That was so long ago at the beginning of summer."

"In a teephone conversation, he said he intended to be friends with you, but you didn't show any signs of wanting to be nice to him, then or very few times after." Martha paused. Sihon shook his head.

Martha continued sensitivity, "So he grew tired of trying to be nice to you, only to be met with hostility."

Sihon sighed. "I'm sorry, Nurse Asquinn-Turehue, but Conrad, or anyone else in that household, did not try to be nice to me."

"Conrad said he and your aunt, and parents asked you to spend the summer with them because your parents regretted the way you were treated when you were with them."

" Perhaps when I first arrived, then Conrad and his followers treated me as if I didn't have feelings."

"You said no one," Martha said. "Did you dad mistreat you?"

"Ignored me is more like it," Sihon said. "Until it came time to take me to the train. Dad drove me to the train station."

"Do you remember what Mr. Cameron said to you?" Martha asked.

"Nurse Asquinn-Turehue, please quite this nonsense and get on with the serious stuff. Crystal is in danger. I know it."

"How did you arrive at that conclusion?"

"It's simple. After Wipinkino and Trevor dropped the hint that I should research black magic, I did so last night. I spent most of that stormy night reading the descriptions in Encyclopedia Britannica."

"What did you find?"

"Nothing but a lot of evil."

Martha nodded. "Black Magic, Voodoo, or Witchcraft, whichever you want to call it, is used to aid the person who practices it get his way with a person."

Sihon fell silent. Martha remained silent. A deep erie silence dominated the room. The clock on the wall beside the desk ticked loudly.   TICK- TOCK, TICK-TOCK.

"Then there is controlling at a distance," Sihon continued.

"How is this accomplished?"

Sihon looked at Martha, wondering if she didn't already know all this.

"Through the voodoo doll."

AS he talked, Sihon became more enthusiastic. "I saw one there the day I arrived. Right on a corner table in the grand entrance way. I thought it was one of Crystal's dolls."

Martha's mouth moved as if she might throw up."How could you think that?"

"Please, remember, I was completely ignorant about evil and spirits," Sihon said. "I know now what it's for. Conrad uses this doll to control me at a distance."

"All he needs is a picture of you, or just talk to the doll as if he were there talking to you," Martha supplied the information. "That alter you witnessed is used for the exact opposite Dad uses his pulpit for. Dad preaches about the love of God, devil worshipers use the alter to call up spirits so they can control a particular person, in this case, you."

"And pins. Pins to jab the doll and I feel the affects through pain in the area he jabbed, irritation, or a tingling in my body."

"You've stumbled into something evil and powerful," Martha said. "it is the same evil forces Dad had to combat when he first brought the family to the James Bay Frontier, as a missionary. Satanism, Devil worship, which ever you prefer."

"But it won't work, Nurse Asquinn-Turehue."

"You can't fight Conrad, or the evil spirits that possess him, rather, on your own. The spirits are more powerful than you and I. Don't even try."

"But I'm a child of God, a child of the King. I've heard sermons by Pastor Asquinn a child of God fights the evil spirits through the use of Jesus's name."

"That's right," Martha agreed.

"Then I'm well equipped to fight the battle with Conrad," Sihon said firmly. He invited me there to his estate assuring me my parents were terribly sorry how they treated me when I was not even three years old."

"I believe you have it all figured out, Sihon."

"When all the time the scheme was to get me under his roof to work on me and get used enough to the life of luxury and fortune enough to want his inheritance. Why, sending me back here is even deception. He did so, and through his voodoo controls my behaviour, so that Martin, Audrey and the girls will tire of my behaviour and send me back in disgrace."

Martha nodded.

"It's not going to work. I have God and a host of guardian angels on my side. Conrad can't help but bow his knees."

PSALMS 44:4&5

44/Thou art my King, Oh God; command deliverance for Jacob.

45/ Through thee we will push down our enemies: through they name we will tread them under that rise up against us.

Martha reached across her desk and took Sihon's hand in hers.

"You won't be alone. The family, Golden Ridge Baptist Chruch is behind you."

The afternoon before the day school started for the fall term, all but Sihon sat at the kitchen table. Wapinkino sat between Kathleen and Eunice, and Trevor sat beside Cassia. Lorne leaned up against the kitchen cupboards. Vanna stood beside him. Each teen had a bottle of soft drink in front of him. The y were not alone. Tadcu sat at the head of the table where Martin usually sat, while Mamcu bustled around the kitchen.

"Court should be over with by now," Olvina said.

"Yeah, Tadcu, when will they be home?"

"Soon, I expect," Tadcu answered.

"Kathleen bring me a plate," Mamcu said.

Kathleen fetched a plate from the cupboard. "Let me do this, please. You sit down and rest."

When Mamcu nodded, Kathleen piled high some cinnamon buns and set the plate on the table.

"These are freshly baked," she said.

"Let me have one," Lorne said and claimed a bun from the top of the pile.

"Out of my way," Lorne said.

"Those look good," Vanna said.

Soon the rest of the group reached for the yummy looking treat.

All the teens were devouring a cinnamon bun when the outside door opened, then closed. Sihon, Ken, Martin, and Audrey stood in the kitchen.

Ken's eyebrows lifted a bit in surprise when he saw all the teen seated, or standing around the room. Sihon's eyes grew wide at the sight of the huge, icing covered treats.

"May I have one, Audrey?"

"Sure," Audrey said.

Sihon dashed to the table, squirmed in beside olvina and soon was eating along with his friends.

"We're just hanging out here, Mr. Asquinn," Lorne said.

"Are you kids happy about school starting tomorrow?" Ken asked.

Groans from most of the kids.

"Definitely, Uncle Ken," Trevor said.

"Find a place to sit down," Audrey said.

"What do we owe the honor of this visit from you to?" Tadcu spoke to Ken.

"Where's you usual assistants?" Lorne ventured to ask.

"Oh, Bradan, Constable Barclay and Murray have their job to do. What I have to say I can say it on my own. I've got some news to pass along, which involves Sihon."

Ken eyed the cinnamon buns on the table and soft drinks in front of each teen. "That brings back memories."

The teen-agers had a good laugh over that.

"By all means have one," Audrey invited.

But Ken declined. "No. But thanks. I'm on duty."

He turned his attention to Sihon. "You look chipper."

"I love being at the table with everyone that's here," Sihon replied brightly. "I feel comfortable and at peace. This peace came to me after I learned not to fight every word that came my way, no matter who it was."

"Good for you," said Ken.

"I know now where I belong," added Sihon. ""I 'm here living with my family. Martin and Audrey are the Mom and Dad of my heart."

"What's the good news?" Cassia asked.

"Yeah, tell us, how did court go?" Eunice asked.

Ken smiled at her to put her at ease. "I checked out Sihon's story about who stole that car. His version is accurate and the girls back him up."

"Does that mean he isn't guilty?" inquired Trevor.

"Yes it does, and the charges against him have been dropped."

The room full of teens greeted this news with much cheering.

"But don't forget you have drinking, driving under age and attacking and hurting Syd, charges to face," Ken pointed out.

"Will he go to jail?" Wipinkino asked.

"The judge doesn't think that will be necessary. He will have to be supervised more closely. The judge ordered Community service for a whole month."

Earlier in the summer I would have rebelled at these words, Sihon thought. *I would have spat out the words 'But wasn't his life miserable enough by being held under such close supervision'? Over the months living with my family and associating with the rest of the Asquinn clan, I look upon rebelling as useless. I realize God had planted this knowledge in me and brought about the change of heart. He knew the man the girls and Trevor called Uncle Ken carried a lot of weight both in the family as Chief of the clan, and in Forest Lake as Chief Superintendent of the police department. In Forest Lake, amongst the police force, his word was law: The man in charge, nothing happened without his ruling. Why fight it? He couldn't fight it. He didn't want to fight it.*

"I will cooperate. I'm tired of being nasty to everyone that's being so nice to me. I don't want to end up like Dad or any of the uncles on his side of the family."

"I can see you've being a lot nicer than you were before," Ken complimented the boy. Sihon felt a warmth that started in his heart spread through his entire being; it made him want to do better.

Sihon paused then plunged into the subject on his mind.

"Ken, while you and Bradan where policemen out west, did you learn to shoot to kill?" inquired Sihon.

Ken didn't look too happy. "Yes we did. I don't like to think of it, but the memory still haunts me some night- and days, too. I didn't actually pull the trigger to kill the man. He had killed, but the commanding officer of the detachment where I worked had caused problems between him and his wife. Both were native, and he a trapper. He killed one Mountie. Thinking it was him that was causing the problem but he turned out to be the wrong man. Naturaly killing the first Mountie caused all the rest to vow to get this man. To shoot him dead. I was sent out to the trapper's cabin to try and persuade him to give himself up willingly. He wouldn't because he knew he wouldn't get any justice."

Ken had to stop. It was several minutes before he could get his emotions under control enough to talk. "I left the trapper's cabin feeling we had become firm friends but also with a premonition that I might not see him alive again."

"What happened?" Sihon wanted to know.

"In the spring an entire army of Mounties went out to the trapper's cabin. He was dead and had been for quite some time. Instead of allowing the Mounties to find and shoot him down like a rabid dog, he shot himself."

"But you didn't have anything to do with your friend's death," Sihon pointed out.

"Indirectly I did. I was with the army of police that went hunting him with only one intention and that was to shoot him."

Olvina shuddered. A shudder followed down the line of teen-agers and over to Lorne.

"I was a member only for a year or two. Neither Uncle Bradan nor I liked it- we loved police work, don't get me wrong- but we were such an incredible long way from home. We missed our families and friends, and especially the church family. In addition to treating us like foreigners, people out west made fun of the music we loved to listen to. When Uncle Bradan and I were your kids' age, there was a television series on and their content was music from down East from Nova Scotia. Uncle Bradan and I loved listening to that show, but in the west they laughed at us for wanting to listen to 'that down east crap' as they called it. I resigned first and came home."

"He joined the Ontario Provincial Police," Eunice said. "For a few years he was the only law enforcement officer around."

"Forest Lake started to grow, and along with this growth the need for more law enforcement officers. The police department continued to expand until it's what it is today and he has the number of officers he does

under his command. Uncle Bradan followed three years later when the department could afford to pay another officer. By then I was already Superintendent."

"But there are MP detachments in Ontario," Sihon pointed out. "Why not just get a job closer?"

"Because what we did is the way we both chose to do it," said Ken, "neither of us have had any regrets. We've said over and over again we're both happier where we are. We've both said many times we feel this is where God wants us to be."

"I'm glad you and Bradan are back in Forest Lake," Sihon said nicely. He wiped a tear from his cheek with the back of his hand. "I don't believe cops are anywhere near what Conrad made me and Crystal believe they are while I was there. If more kids had men like you and Bradan to look up to, maybe they would turn out better."

"That's the way I, and Bradan, feel about it too Sihon," Ken said gently. "We feel we lost a lot the years we were away from here. But I honestly believe I can say this for both of us. We've gained back those empty years by hearing you say what you just did."

There was a break in the policeman's voice as he uttered the last sentence.

Sihon looked around at his circle of friends and said with heartfelt words. "Kids like you guys are fortunate to have role models like Ken and Bradan. The only ones that have to worry are the crooked people on the wrong side of the law, both young and old. Kirby and Cora said some unkind things about the two of you the night of the crash; and I believed them all. I want to be one that doesn't have to worry. I intend to cooperate to the best of my ability with everyone but sometimes I feel both you and Bradan hate me."

The seasoned, veteran police officer glanced at the boy, surprised. Ken went to the boy and rested his hands on his shoulders. "Hate is a strong word, Sihon," he said tolerantly. "None of us are capable of that emotion. I care about you, don't doubt that for a minute. I'm sure I can speak for Bradan, too."

"How do I know?" Sihon asked sincerely. "You and I aren't together in the same room very long and we're exchanging angry words."

"You have to learn to control your demons," said Ken.

"Uncle Ken doesn't tolerate rudeness from any person, even grown men," Trevor said. "He does have a high moral code of ethics, godly conduct, and lives them."

"The night of the crash," began Ken. "It didn't have to be me who accompanied Sergeant Turehue on patrol that night. Two other police officers could have been dispatched, which would have been more in character for me to do. Instead I agreed to accompany him and Constable Barclay, along with Murray. And yes I did try to make them believe I was going out on a cold, dark, and wet night for my brother, but Bradan knew I was concerned about you also, Sihon."

"Really? You two are awesome." Tears surfaced and spilled over onto his cheeks. "Will I ever learn how to behave properly, again? I always seem to end up humiliating everybody and making them angry with me."

"You can and will," Ken said. He still stood behind his chair, hIs arms around him now.

"With God's help," Sihon completed the sentence.

Sihon was much pleased when Ken squeezed his shoulder and said softly. "You're doing all right. Keep it up."

Uncle Ken released Sihon's hand and stepped away from the chair, "Sorry, everyone, but I must leave now and get back to work."

Martin and Audrey escorted the officer to the door and after the door shut behind him, shuffled into the front room where they found more comfortable seats than the kitchen chairs. They could still hear conversation in the kitchen.

"I think you should be going out on your own and start remaking friends," Eunice said."You've been here long enough to have made dozens more friends than you have,"

Sihon swallowed some orange soft drink.

"There's lots fourteen year old boys," Wipinkino told Sihon. "It's all in how you treat people."

Sihon promised, "I'll work on treating people nicer. I'll start with you,Wipinkino. Please forgive me and let's be friends."

"That happened so long ago I'd forgotten about it," Wipinkino said, considering past events. "Apology accepted and we're friends."

"It's none of my business, but you've missed a lot of church this summer," Lorne pointed out.

Sihon nodded but looked sad.

"Phoebe and I will help you with church and what you missed ," Olvina said,"Won,t we, phoebe?"

"Aboslutely," Phoebe agreed.

"We'll even pay you two for tutoring Sihon," Martin said.

Olvina and Phoebe's eyebrows raised, so surprised were we to hear what their Dad said.

"Pay us?" Phoebe squeaked.

"You deserve it," Martin said. "All your friends have paying jobs. And I realize how incomplete you've both felt all summer because you didn't have a job that paid wages."

"Cool," Olvina said.

"Thanks Dad," Olvina and Phoebe said in unison.

"Martin, is the system Tim set up for me still in effect?" Sihon asked. Tim was another of Martin's brothers and assistant Pastor to Pastor Asquinn. At thity years of age, he and his wife had two children, Edwin age ten and Margaret, age eight.

"Oh yes," Martin said. "We can continue that."

Sihon said, "And I want money taken from that and given to Syd to pay for his bike that I destroyed."

There were gasps from all around the room.

"That's generous of you," Martin said.

"Starting tomorrow, school, work as well as Sunday School and church will keep me busy," Sihon said. "I truly enjoy Church and I feel there is a huge gap over the summer.""

"There is," Audrey said.

"I can get required material right now," Sihon said. "And you girls can get started right away."

He got up and strode over to some shelves along one side of the front room walls. He returned to the kitchen table with a large, blue hard covered book and a larger soft covered exercise book containing questions. He set the hard covered book in front of Olvina and the green book in front of Phoebe. The rest of the girls, and the boys, rose to go outside. Martin and Audrey retreated to the living-room, leaving Sihon, Olivina and Phoebe alone at the table.

"This is a study on Genesis. Read through the chapter, then at the end of each chapter there's questions; answer these questions all through the book."

It seemed to Sihon that only an ahour had passed when Audrey came back to the kitchen and said, "Bedtime now. Remember, you have to get up early. School starts tomorrow."

A pale light glowed show on the horizon the next morning. Sihon walked along the beach, a plastic garbage bag in one hand and a long wooden handle with a hook on the end in the other. Coming to some discarded candy bar wrappers, he pooked the wrapper up with the hook and dropped the tinfoil into the garbage bag.

"That's my time for community service today," he said to the sea gulls flying all around him

At home, Sihon took off his shoes in the entrance way, stole across the kitchen and towards his and Lorne's bedroom. At the boys' room he stopped by the closed door and listened. None stirred so Lorne must still be asleep.

Sihon pushed open the door, "Get up, Lorne. School starts today, remember?"

Lorne moaned and turned over on his side facing the wall and snuggled deeper into his covers and pretended to sleep. "Let me sleep," Lorne said.

"Get up."

Lorne opened his eyes. "I don't want to go to school. I wish school was never invented."

Sihon smiled. He said, "You just can't quit going to school."

"Yes I can."

"Not for a few years," Sihon pointed out. "Time to get up."

Lornels pushed himself up on his elbows and faced his room mate, sleepily. "I'll get you for this."

"I wanted to make sure you weren't late for their first day of school."

"Okay, Okay." Lorne pushed back the covers, and swung his legs over the edge of the bed. Feet sought slippers, and then Lorne jumped Sihon from behind. With a yelp of surprise, Sihon fell onto his own bed. Shouting and laughter resulted as the boys play wrestled on the bed.

It stopped suddenly when Martin entered the room. Sihon noticed immediately his tight lips. He knew from experience not to push Martin any farther. Sihon wrestled free of Lorne and sat up.

"Try and hurry please, boys. We're running a bit behind schedule and the teachers don't wait," Martin said.

"We'll hurry, Mr. Asquinn," Lorne promised.

The girls were already dressed and finished eating by the time Sihon and Lorne reached the breakfast table. Lorne filled his bowl with cereal and quickly gulped down a mouthful or two.

Olvina put her dirty dishes in the sink, followed by her sisters.

"Mom, we've finished our chores. May we leave for school now?"

"Yes," Audrey replied.

Lorne quickly rose from the table, "Wait, I'm coming too."

A little while later Sihon stood by the ally way running between two rows of houses. He could see Brian, Raymond, and Syd walking. Sihon waved and the three brothers waved back. The boys started to run towards each other. They met at the boardwalk leading up to the school.

"Syd, I'm terribly sorry about what I did with your bicycle," Sihon apologized.

"That's okay," Syd said. "Dad recovered the bike for me. It wasn't in very deep water."

"I want us to be friends," Sihon said.

"Sure, why not?" Syd and Sihon shook hands.

"Hurry up you two," Brian said.

"Yeah. Over the summer two new teachers were hired," Raymond said. "I'm curious to see who's teaching grades one to eight." He ran on ahead.

Sihon stopped at a door and knocked. It was opened by a small, slight man with sandy colored hair and brown eyes.

""I'm Mr. Fraser, your home room teacher."

" I'm Sihon Weistien."

"I know who you are," Mr. Fraser sad. "Forest Lake is a small enough community for everyone to know everyone else. Welcome, Asquinn,." Mr. Fraser said kindly. "Do come in, please."

Inside the classroom and the door shut once more, Mr. Fraser said. Find a place to sit."

Sihon looked round for a place to sit. He saw Raymond who was seated, the desk beside him empty

"Anyone sitting here?"

"There is now, you."

With school to attend, community service both before and, after school and the first bible lessons approaching, Sihon had lots to keep him occupied. More important, he found he was quite intent on learning.

One school morning he woke up early. Looking at his clock on the nightstand, he noticed the hands were at seven o'clock, so the alarm hadn't gone off yet. He pushed back the covers, went to the closet and picked out the clothes he would wear to school. He was doing up the last button on his shirt when the alarm rang. By the time Audrey arrived to shake
him awake, he was standing by his mirror combing his hair.

"You're awake early."

"And starved. When do we eat?"

"We would eat sooner if you would set the table."

"I will." Sihon set his comb aside and hugged Audrey.

"What was that for?"

"You deserve a big hug for being so kind to me. For the first time this summer I feel loved and secure."

Audrey, brushed the corner of one eye with the sleeve of her robe. "Why thank you, dear. I'm glad you're starting to feel at home with us again."

She left the room, followed by Sihon. In the kitchen he joined the girls. In the bathroom, Martin's shaver hummed.

Olvina took down some dinnerplates from the kitchen cupboards, handed these to Phoebe who carried them to the table and set places on the table. Olvina followed with more. Cassia and Kathleen placed silverware by the plates, while Eunice set a container of juice in the middle of the table.

Audrey placed boxes of ceral beside the milk container. The noise of her husband's shaver stopped.

"Breakfast is ready, Martin, dearest," Audrey called.

"I'll be there in a sec," Martin answered.

Martin came to the table and everyone sat down. Soon plates or bowls were filled and the family ate.

The school day over, that evening Olvina knocked on Sihon's bedroom door.

"Come in."

Olvina pushed open the door and stepped inside. Sihon lay on his back on his bed, earphones plugged into his ears, listening to tapes

"I thought I'd find you here," Olvina said.

Sihon nodded but kept on listening to the music.

"Are you going to listen to that all evening?" Olvina demanded after a five-minute wait. "I thought you wanted to learn all you could about the bible."

"I am. Mamcu gave me these tapes to listen to."

"It's Uncle Ken and Uncle Bradan singing; are they awesome or what?"

"Yes," Sihon said. "Tadcu also gave me a dramatized version of the bible to listen to. He said I was listening to too much rock music."

"And he was right," Olvina agreed. She shouted to be heard. "Sihon, I want to introduce you to our first lesson this evening."

Sihon shut off the music. Olvina glanced around the bedroom. "Is it true you are in the same room as Joanne?"

Joanne Turehue was the youngest daughter of Bradan and Martha

Turehue. Shannon, the oldest girl, was sixteen and in grade eleven. The oldest boys, Gerald and Lyle were away at police college.

"That's right."

Sihon got up off the bed. Olvina led them out to the kitchen where they drew out chairs and sat down.

Pastor Asquinn and his were already seated and waiting in the living room with Martin and Audrey. Tadcu sat in the front room in an easy chair, but could hear what was being said in at the kitchen table.

"I'm really glad there aren't many in the class," Sihon joked. "Crowds make me nervous. What am I learning today?"

"About creation," Olvina said.

"Creation? I already know about creation. The world began with a big bang and we've all evolved from apes." He grinned as he said it.

"Sit down and listen. From now on we don't pay any attention to what theology teaches. We never learned about evolution either in school or church."

Olvina patted the bible on the table in front of her. "We learn and go by what this says."

Anger boiled within Sihon. He started to feel irritated. He thought Olvina sneered at him. She thought him ignorant. Her family thought my family are big snobs! It didn't seem like she thinks I'm much of a Christian if she thinks I don't know the origins of man and creation.

Instead of letting the evil spirits get the better of him, Sihon pushed himself to his feet and moved away from the table.

Sihon's actions brought Olvina to her feet. His actions also brought them in the living-room, and from upstairs, into the kitchen. Everyone watched, hushed, as Sihon said loudly, "Oh, no, not this time. You have no control over me. Jesus and His angels are stronger than you. Get thee behind me, Satan. In Jesus' name I command you."

Immediately, Sihon felt a presence leave his body. He sat down again, at peace. There was a sigh from those grouped around in various spots. Kathleen, followed by Cassia, Phoebe and Eunice, walked up to Sihon.

"Good for you," Kathleen said.

"How do you feel?" Eunice asked.

Tadcu touched Olvina's shoulder. "I don't believe Sihon needs to be taught the Bible. Not the way he just quoted scripture and chased the evil away."

Not one person tired to look superior. Their faces showed nothing but kindness and concern, wanting to help him.

Chapter Ten
Thanksgiving

Cassia handed Sihon a letter.

Sihon took the letter. He looked at the return address.

"Who's it from?" Olvina asked eagerly.

"It's from Dad," Sihon said. He tore open the envelope and read.

"What's new at home?" Phoebe said when he looked up from the single sheet.

"Nothing. What about it Martin, Audrey? May my Dad come to visit?"

The five sisters exchanged glances. Audrey said to her husband.

"Do you suppose that is wise?"

"For how long?' she asked when no one commented.

"He's talking about a visit over the Thanksgiving Day weekend."

"I don't see why a visit wouldn't be all right," Martin said.

"That sounds reasonable," Audrey agreed.

"Great!" exclaimed Sihon. "Oh wow!t. I'm going to study all my subjects and Dad will be real proud of me."

"He should be, anyway," Audrey said.

"Mr. Fraser says you are doing really well in your first year of high school," Martin praised the boy.

Sihon jumped to his feet excitedly. "I'll send a letter off right away."

"You know where the writing material is," Cassia said.

"I'll do it. I'll do it." There was new light in Sihon's hazel eyes.

He stood up and retrieved a writing pad and pen, returned to the kitchen table and started to write. The rest remained in the living-room.

Dear Dad, Sihon began and his concentration was wholly on writing the letter. *It's me, your son, Sihon.*

He could almost hear the silence from Conrad if he happened to read this letter.

I'm fine. I got your letter today. Martin, Audrey and the girls think it's a good idea, you coming for a visit.

Sihon felt so happy he almost got up and danced a jig, pen in one hand and all. How can I be so happy about Dad coming for a visit? Why do I still call him Dad? He guessed it was because he and his Dad were closer than he ever realized and it was almost impossible to separate blood relatives.

That's why I'm writing; I'm so happy. I can't believe I'll be seeing you in ten days. It's a long time since we've seen each other. I like my new section of the school. It's really cool. My schoolteachers, Mr. Fraser and Martin, are real nice and I don't mind Tadcu or his daughter, Nurse Martha Asquinn-Turehue, as my psychologist. I'm even beginning to have some real good discussions with Ken and Bradan. Just so that will know, policemen are my friends.

I had this crazy notion that maybe some of the kids would laugh at me. They don't. They're all so nice to me, and want to be helpful. Chiefly, the boys in my Sunday school class are my classmates.

Sihon could hear Conrad's grunt if he read the last sentence.

A few nights later Sihont was again at the table eating a meal with the family. Half way through his meat and vegetables the phone rang. "I'll answer it," he said, and got up from the table. He returned a few minutes later, smiling. "That was Dad. His train arrives here at Forest Lake eight o'clock a.m."

"What day?" Olvina asked.

"Saturday." Sihon said.

The Saturday morning Mr. Weistien was to get there, arrived. Sihon went with Martin in the car to meet the tain at the station. Audrey and the girls waited at home. The five sisters were lined up at front room window that looked out onto Golden Ridge Circle Drive, and across to the railroad tracks. Audrey kept busy by sewing a patch on an old torn pair of Sihon's jeans.

The passenger train Mr. Weistien arrived on chugged and whistled its way along the railroad tracks only yards from the front lawns.

"I wish it were more than just my Dad coming." Sihon said.

"Who else would you like to come?"

"Crystal," Sihon said wistfully. "Conrad or Lillian would never come to visit me."

Sihon watched as the train approached the station.

The long train pulled to a stop at the station.

"Sihon, are you crying?" Martin said.

Sihon did the best to hide the fact he was crying by continuing to stand gazing at the enormous engine. He pretended to be looking for the coach his dad would descend from, but really he was fighting back tears that threatened to spill open like floodgates.

"At first when I realized I didn't want what Conrad offered me, I felt numb and didn't feel anything. Now I'm fighting to control the hurt and rejection. Oh, where is he?" he asked impatiently.

"He will be here. Be patient."

The coach door opened, and the conductor, dressed in a blue uniform, stepped down. He placed an extra step beneath the regular steps. Mr. Weistien appeared and climbed down onto the cinder platform.

The conductor picked up the extra step, climbed aboard and the train chugged away.

Sihon dashed towards Mr. Weistein. Martin followed. Sihon squealed and hurled himself at Mr. Weistien and embraced him tightly. Mr. Weistien let his luggage slide from his hand. As he and the boy before him drew apart, Mr. Weistien said, "Conrad, Lillian and Crystal will arrive later by car. Lillian hates traveling by train. She says they travel too slowly."

"Where's Mrs. Weistien?" Martin asked. "We were all looking forward to meeting her."

"She can't come here," Mr. Weistien answered. "Relatives of hers invited her to their place for Thanksgiving."

"Dad, why don't you just say it. The woman with you now is not my mother. Where is Mom?"

Sihon's father looked at the toes of his polished leathershoes. When he looked again at Sihon, he asked. "How did you know?"

"I saw all the pictures recording the Cameron history in the third story room."

Mr. Weistien drew a deep breath. "You what? You snooped around Conrad's private rooms?"

"I sure did. Where's Mom?"

Mr. Weistien couldn't look at his son. At last he got the courage to say, "Your Mother left me a long time ago. She doesn't intend on coming back."

Mr. Weistien turned to Martin. He held a hand out to Martin who took the offered hand and the two shook.

"It's so-o-o-o-o nice to see you, Nigel."

"You're looking good, Martin."

"Let's get your baggage loaded and head home," Martin said.

Sihon looked at his father's baggage. "Why did you bring so many suitcases and trunks?"

Martin grabbed a couple of suitcases and Sihon a couple more, and led the way to Martin's station wagon. Mr. Weistien's luggage was put in the trunk. Trunks that wouldn't fit in the car trunk, were shoved into the back seat. Sihon climbed into the back seat beside his father's baggage, his father in the front seat with Martin driving.

Mr. Weistien turned to look at Sihon. "I feel you should be told this. Sihon, Conrad and Lillian will be leaving Crystal with some relative here. The authorities have decided they not fit to bring up their children."

"Good," Sihon said.

Martin came to his driveway and turned the car onto the gravel. Soon all were inside.

"Nigel, meet my wife, Audrey. Audrey this is Nigel Weistien. Meet our precious quints, Olvina, Phoebe, Cassia, Kathleen and Eunice."

Audrey and the girls shook hands with this stranger, making him feel welcome.

Sihon took his father by the hand. " I'll show you where you sleep. Is that okay, Audrey, Martin?"

"Certainly," Audrey said.

"And then you can make yourself useful by carrying Mr. Weistien's bagge inside," Martin said.

"I will."

Sihon steered him to the guestroom she would occupy while visiting.

The next morning, Thanksgiving Day, Sihon stirred beneath the covers. A sound awakened him. Someone stood by his bed. Sihon looked towards the sound.

"Crystal."

"Hurry and get up. Dad, Mom and I have already arrived. We'll be eating dinner, soon."

Sihon now smelled turkey cooking, gravy being made, apple pies baking in the oven and of biscuits.

"Oh, now I remember. Last night Dad and I stayed up very late talking and catching up on the news. Today a huge crowd of aunts, and uncles, and cousins are gathering here for Thanksgiving Day dinner."

"Hurry and get dressed and come into the kitchen," Crystal said and went from the room.

Sihon flung back his covers, sprang out of bed and started to dress. Finished dressing, he rushed into the front room then the kitchen where everything waited nicely at the table. He paused by a corner of the room where the girls were grouped together with Murray, Gerald, Kirk and Lyle.

"How is Police College going?" Sihon.

"It's fantastic," answered Lyle.

Kirk assured his cousin. "I'd never be anything else but a police officer."

Gerald assured Sihon. "I love it."

"I love it too," said Murray. "I enjoy my studies now that I'm truly in class."

Morley and Gay walked by, him with an arm around her waist and her with one arm around his waist. Then Sihon saw Conrad Lillian and tried welcoming him with a wide, happy smile, but Conrad only looked down at his shiny spotless shoes.

Pastor Asquinn walked into the room. Ken, Charlotte and the boys were already seated next to him at the table. "We can all be seated. We're all here and can enjoy this wonderful food now. I will ask my youngest son, Ken to say the grace."

There was a rush to find seats. The younger children were seated at a separate table, but Sihon scrambled to make sure he got a seat with his father. He wondered why he should have bothered as Conrad and Lillian sat nearby. Both acted as if he didn't know Sihon was anywhere around, let alone right beside them.

After all were seated, Conrad reached for a bowl of vegetables and started spooning them onto his plate.

Sihon whispered, "We don't eat until we say grace here."

Conrad shot the boy a 'you're crazy' look but stopped what he was doing and bowed his head along with the rest.

Ken stood up and began. *"We all have a lot to be thankful for. Dear Father in heaven, we want to thank you for the wonderful fellowship of family, this fine Thanksgiving day and the wonderful food we are about to partake in as well as all the blessings and prosperity throughout the year. Amen."*

Sihon, along with the men and some other boys, echoed Ken's amen and the feasting began.

Sihon turned to speak to his father. "I'm really, really glad you're here today."

Mr. Weistien pressed his son's knee. "So am I."

Conrad ignored him and continued to fork gravy, potatoes and turkey meat into his mouth. Sihon wiped a tear from one cheek. He felt Conrad's rejection keenly.

"You aren't sulking, I hope," Conrad said sideways, not looking straight at Sihon . "You will have to toughen up."

"He misses both of you," Martin said.

"It's beastly how you treat him," Audrey added her thoughts.

Sihon's Dad stepped in and backed her up. "Sihon is the best thing that happened to me."

Sihon's Dad snorted, and scratched the top of his head.

"Isn't Crystal the best thing that happened to you and Lillian?" Martin asked.

"That's easy for all of you to say, you haven't had to live with her for the past eleven years."

Martin was about to make some remark, but Conrad threw down his knife and fork, pushed back his chair and said to his wife, and daughter. "Come on, Lillian, Crystal. I don't have to stay here and listen to this."

Crystal protested. "But we only just started to eat."

She was having a great time talking and laughing with her cousins on either side of her.

"What a delightful child," Audrey commented. "Ken if it hasn't been decided where she is to stay, I vote she stay with us."

"And I second that," Mamcu said.

There were shouts of total agreement from almost everyone else in the house.

Martin looked at Audrey and smiled. "It's been decided, darling. The little girl stays with us. How about sealing the occasion with a kiss?"

"Gladly."

"And the rest of you are witnesses to this agreement," Martin said. Sihon clapped and whistled as Martin's lips covered Audrey's and they held the kiss for many long minutes. Soon everyone at the table clapped and made noises. Audrey sat breathless by the time the embrace ended.

"We'll have our own meal at home," Conrad declared.

"Have you forgotten home is 600 miles away," Audrey asked. Conrad pushed back his chair and started towards the table where Crystal sat. He grabbed her by one hand and pulled her out of her chair. Crystal cried.

"I want to stay, Daddy."

Sihon watched in shock as Conrad dragged his family away from the table and headed towards the door.

Ken, and then Bradan, trailed by Morley, was on his feet in a flash and followed the family through the kitchen and then outside. Sihon leaped up from his chair and followed.

"Aren't you forgetting something, Conrad?"

"What am I forgetting, Ken?"

Gently Ken lifted Crystal into his arms. Audrey, with Martin beside her, stepped up to him and held out her arms for the little girl. "I'll take her inside. She shouldn't have to listen to all this."

Ken relinquished Crystal without argument. He reminded Conrad when the three were inside. "Crystal is not yours anymore. You are not taking her with you. The judge said she was to be delivered to us Thanksgiving Day. Remember what day this is?"

Conrad's protest was emotionless. "I've never done anything to her."

"How do we know that?"

"She's the joy of my heart." Conrad's cry did nothing to convince those standing by that he meant it.

Ken said firmly. "She stays. It's already been decided."

"By whom?'

"The authorities," said Bradan.

Conrad said spitefully. His eyes shot red fire at Ken. "That means you, I suppose."

Ken would not be intimidated. He said firmly. "It's been decided."

Conrad stared at Ken for a few moments, but Ken stared unwaveringly back. Conrad looked away.

Lillian said "Give me one good reason why she's being taken away from us."

Ken pointed out. "I don't have to give reasons for my decisions but I will. You are not fit parents; that has been illustrated with Crystal just now and Sihon while he visited you and Lillian at Cameron Estate. Where do you think he got all his evil characteristics?"

Conrad said without feeling. "Oh all right, Ken, have it your way; you always did, even when we were boys."

Bradan corrected him. "Not always. He had his way only when he was right, and most of the time he's right. I still correct him when I think he's wrong; not only that but our church regulates his behavior. If a member thinks he's behaving anyway that doesn't bring honor to God, then we let him know about it."

"Who are you?"

"Kurt, even you must have figured out by now who I am."

"No, I haven't."

Sihon realized Conrad knew who Bradan was and between him and Ken, Conrad looked mighty nervous. He turned to Mrs. Cameron. "We might as well go Lillian. We obviously aren't welcome around here."

Sihon said to Lillian. "I won't say good-bye, because I pray it isn't that."

Conrad scoffed. "You're starting to sound too much like the Asquinn-Olverton and Turehue side of the family. Praying indeed!"

Lillian hugged Sihon.

"Be sure to write," sniffed Sihon.

"Come on," Conrad snapped at Mrs. Cameron. "Let's get out of here."

Conrad turned to Sihon's father, "You, too."

Mr. Weistien shook his head. "I'm staying here in Forest Lake."

"You are coming with us," Conrad said.

"I'm not."

Conrad's stony features seemed to grow stonier and he reached out to grab his brother's shoulder. Sihon sprang between Conrad and his father.

"You leave my Dad alone. We honour God in this family and we don't need people like you."

At the word 'GOD' Conrad seemed to wilt and he stepped backwards, away from this slim teen-ager. He turned to his wife.

Mrs. Cameron had not been quick enough for her husband's liking in saying good-byes. His final humiliation came when his half-brother refused to obey him. He started flinging angry words at her the moment she joined him by the car where he had unloaded Crystal's suitcases.

Out of the corner of his eye, Sihon noticed Tammy suddenly bend over as if in pain. She grabbed Murray for support. Audrey was right at her side and with her on one side and Murray on the other, Tammy into the house.

"Maybe you would prefer to stay with Sihon and Crystal and our other many loved ones?"

" I was just saying good bye to them. I don't know when we'll be seeing them again."

Conrad said furiously, "You won't have to worry about seeing them again, because you won't be leaving them. I'm going home alone."

With those words he quickly got behind the wheel of the car. Sihon caught a glimpse of the man's face. His heart ached for him who he once called uncle as he saw much pain in the man's eyes and his face distorted with hurting.

Sihon look behind him and up at Martin. He knew he'd seen remorse and regret on Conrad Cameron's face, also.

Instead of turning around and entering the street properly, Conad plunged the vehicle forward. He jumped the sleek sports car across the little hill and into the parking lot.

Ken winced at the memory when he, at the age of nineteen, and newly married, and about to set out on his honeymoon with his beloved new bride, did the very same thing.

In his side vision Sihon saw Audrey appear at the doorway and in his subconscious mind, heard her words, "Martha, come quickly. The baby's coming."

Martha separated from her husband and rushed towards the house.

Conrad roared into Circle Drive and drove west, but not before Mrs. Cameron could get in the seat beside him. He then turned the car westward along Golden Ridge Circle Drive and, with squealing tires, took off at a much too high a speed, for out of town.

"He won't get very far if he insists on driving like that," Sihon said.

Ken agreed. "Bradan go after him, arrest him and lock him up. Take with you whoever you wish."

Bradan turned to his sons, Gerald and Lyle. "Come on, we'll intercept that mad driver and arrest him. We'll use my car, Ger."

Sihon said to Bradan, "I must get in this morning's community service time."

Sihon retrieved a garbage bag, a rake and started towards the road.

He'd picked up a few discarded pop bottles and candy wrappers before coming to the crossing by the bay in front of the store.

He saw Bradan cut off Conrad's careless dash for out of town just before rounding the corner by the railroad crossing in front of van Ladislav's restaurant. Sihon threw down the partially filled garbage bag and rake and started at a run to join the activity.

Bradan, followed by Gerald and Lyle, leaped out of the car and dashed for Conrad's car just as he opened the door and stepped out.

Sihon joined the three, and watched with a smile on his face, as Bradan slapped handcuffs on Conrad. "You're under arrest Conrad Cameron."

"What for?"

"For speeding and endangering other people's lives. Now you will have to spend three days in jail. Ken doesn't come back on duty until Monday. By then you won't even own that beauty of a car you were so bent on wrecking."

"You don't know that," Conrad said defiantly

What an arrogant man, Sihon thought.

"Oh, I do," Bradan said. "As commanding officer of the Forest lake detachment of the Police Department, I know we have men down south raiding your casino as we speak; it was me that set it all in motion. The casino will be shut down, and along with losing your livelihood you will lose your grand house along with the BMW car, and family van. Those huge impressive figures that make up your bank account will be nothing but zeros. You're nothing but a pathetic vagabond, Conrad- you own nothing. Your operating license has been revoked."

"You're Bradan Turehue," Conrad said pretending that recognition had just come to him.

"Yes, I am."

"Ken's lifelong, loyal sidekick; how nice to meet you again," Conrad said smoothly.

"It's funny you should remember me at this very moment. I'm more than his sidekick. There's a big thing there called a bondage from God between us, but you wouldn't know anything about that, would you? You've never had a true loyal friend in all your life, Kurt. Remember, the kids called you Kurt when we were in school."

To Sihon's great satisfaction, Conrad flinched at the memory of using the shortened Kurt as a kid in grade school. When he entered high school, he ordered every kid to be call him Conrad, his full name

Bradan continued. "The only ones that are loyal to you are the men you pay great wads of money to be true; and then it's only as long as you're paying them."

Conrad merely grunted at these words.

Bradan was unshakable. "You knew all along who I am. You aren't going to change a lifelong bond with that smooth talking silver tongue of yours to swing me over onto your side. If I were you I'd have a change of attitude pretty quick, before I slap bribery charges along with the many other tabs you will have to reckon with."

"I will see that those charges don't stick. "I won't stay closed for long."

Bradan held a different view. "We think so. We know you're also connected with Hell's Angels and their dirty drug trafficking."

"Oh Conrad, when will you stop?" Lillian said. "How many lives will you destroy before you're content? This time it's your own daughters-not to mention mine."

Bradan looked at Gerald. "I have a job for you."

"What's that, Dad?"

"You take this man and lock him up, immediately. Use his car and then have it impounded. I'll phone ahead and let them know you're coming. Here's the keys, get to it."

"Then can I go back to Martin's and finish my thanksgiving dinner?" Gerald asked.

This made Sihon smile

"Yes, you can."

Gerald started towards the car with Conrad walking ahead of him. Suddenly he stopped and stared at the vehicle. "What a beautiful car. Dad, this is the perfect vehicle for us to travel back and forth to college."

"It sure is," agreed Lyle.

"The way things are now we depend on another driver to get us home," Lyle said. "He doesn't always want to go straight home like we do. Sometime he leaves us sitting for hours while he drinks in a pub. And with our own transportation we would be able to travel more comfortably with our families."

"I get the idea. We should be able to afford to buy this car for the four of you to use."

"Thanks Dad."

Bradan specified. "Ger, you and Lyle will have to prove yourself a responsible driver before I sign anything."

"Sure, Dad," the brothers agreed.

Bradan helped Conrad into the back seat of his own car and Gerald drove away with him. Bradan turned to Mrs. Cameron. "We'll find a place for you. Do you have relatives close by?"

"I have a sister in Lakeview."

"Then my son and I will drive you there."

"Thank you. The three of you have been so nice to me."

"Our pleasure, Ma'am," Lyle said.

"Don't count on seeing your husband too soon, nor will your daughter see her father in the near future," Bradan told Lillian.

Before Bradan could get behind the wheel, Sihon stepped up to him.

"I wonder how long it will be before those two split? Bradan, is this what backlash means? Conrad lost his daughter, and wife, by the looks of it?".

"That's exactly what happened. Conrad got what he deserved."

"He got what he deserves without Dad innocently being arrested along with him," Sihon said. He felt oddly detached from it all, as if it wasn't happening to him. Bradan touched his shoulder, and said kindly, "Go, finish what you were doing."

Bradan slid behind the wheel, started the engine and drove off.

Sihon turned to go back to tidying up.

Badan, Gerald and Lyle arrived back. Sihon sat down at the table with them.

"I believe I deserve some more goodies after an hour of community service," he said. "Picking up behind other people works up an appetite. May I, Mom."

"Sure, go ahead," Audrey answered.

Sihon and the men finished their turkey and trimmings dinner. Bradan pushed away his plate from in front of him. "Thanks, Audrey. I'm stuffed."

Gerald, did the same. "That was a delicious meal you and the girls prepared, ma'am. I can't eat another bite.

"Me neither," Lyle agreed.

Audrey wiped a tear of gratitude from the corner of one eye with the end of her apron. "The three of you deserve a good meal after what you did to help out Ken. You're all great men, but I believe Murray is going to be great leader and an exceptional policeman after his training, just like his Dad."

Lyle and Gerald received these compliments graciously, having known all their lives that it was so.

Bradan said agreeable."I believe you are right, Audrey."

Bradan pushed back his chair and got to his feet and his sons followed his example. Bradan, Gerald and Lyle right behind him, moved to the living-room. Sihon remained seated at the table,in the kitchen alone with Audrey until Martin entered the room, pulled a chair away from the table and sat down.

Martin and Audrey entered the kitchen. Martin held Crystal

tenderly in his arms where the little girl wrapped her arms around him, head resting contentedly against his shoulder, eyes closed, showing she trusted him completely. Audrey kissed her lightly on the forehead.

"I see you three are bonding," Sihon said. Martin nodded agreement.

"Maybe Crystal will like to visit the animals at the zoo," Audrey said.

Crystal,bright blue eyes opened, she wriggled to get free. Martin allowed her to slide gently to her feet on the floor.

Audrey squatted to be more at Crystal's level. "How about it dear, would you like to see the animals at the zoo?"

"There's white tailedd Deer, red foxes, and wolves, to name only a few," Martin said.

"I sure would Mommy, Daddy. When can we go?"

"Right away," Martin said.

"Can Sihon come, too?"

"Sure," Audrey said.

"Mommy? Daddy?" Sihon questioned with raised eyebrows.

"Shuuuuu. She can call me Daddy all she wishes."

Mamcu and Tadcu were the first couple Martin, Audrey, Sihon and Crystal met when they returned from the zoo an hour and a hald later.

Crystal rushed to her grandmother and hugged her, then her grandfather.

"What did you see at the zoo" Mamcu asked.

"Just like Daddy said, deer, a wolf and a fox," Crystal replied.

"We're going home now," Tadcu said. "Martin, Audrey, and the girls, this was truly a memorial Thanksgiving Day. The food was superb."

"And the fellowship with other Christians of like faith, a blessing," Vincent said.

Morley cleared his throat. "Everyone, we have an announcement to make."

"What's that?" Martin asked.

Morley made the announcement loud and clear. "Gay has agreed to marry me."

Gay-Anne showed off her engagement ring: first to her own parents, Eric and June, then to all in the room.

"You will have to give either Tim or me an announcement to read in church for this Sunday," Tadcu said. "Other church members will be overjoyed to hear about another wedding."

"We will," Morley said.

There was a stirring as someone appeared in the guestroom doorway.

Eunice squealed with delight.

"The baby's here," Kathleen said.

"How wonderful," Phoebe said.

"I can't wait to see the baby," Olvina added.

Cassia was just as joyful as her sisters," "I can't wait to hold the baby."

"What's all the fuss," Sihon asked. "It's just a baby."

Tammy and Murray were met by a mass of relatives and friends eager to see the baby. Murray remained beside his wife, his embrace including the newborn cuddled in her arms. His head was bent over as he gazed down at their newborn daughter. The baby laughed and cooed happily back.

"It's a girl," Murray said to the eager waiters.

"Can we see her" Cassia asked eagerly.

"You sure can," said the mother, smiling

Those that had just entered the room admired the child.

"What a beautiful babe!" exclaimed Charlotte.

When it was his turn to admire the tot, Ken tenderly took the baby in his arms and gazed down into her tiny face. The newborn responded by smiling and gurgling happily at him.

Ken, then Charlotte, then Sihon kissed the ever so tiny forehead before passing her.

Martin and Martha had to have their turn in holding her. Martha returned her to her mother. "Have you named her?"

"We've already named her. There's no doubt about it," Murray said. "This is Joy Charlotte Tamar Asquinn."

Sihon walked up to where his father, Martin and Audrey sat, "May I have a hug, too?"

Audrey said, agreeable, "Sure."

Sihon included, Martin, Audrey and his father in his hug.

"I'm glad you're staying Dad," Sihon said."I'm glad Crystal's staying with Eric and June."

"This way she's almost next door," Martin said."You're welcome to go over to Eric and June's and visit her anytime."

Sihon smiled at him.

"I will. I'm sorry for what I've said earlier. Please forgive me. I think you are all a very awesome people."

Martin and Audrey received the boy's praise graciously. "Thank you. I forgive you."

Bradan and Martha softly joined her twin's family. She drew the boy to her and hugged him.

"Don't think Conrad and his evil spirits are through with you, yet," she cautioned. "They will be back."

"But I'll be ready for them," Sihon said.

Sihon turned to his father.

"Dad, I love you." Sihon stepped back and stood beside Martin and Audrey. "But Martin is the Dad of my heart, and Audrey the Mom of my heart."

" I still love you son. I wish from the bottom of my heart that circumstances had of been different and I could have raised you. I won't try to take you back now. I currently don't have my own place to live, or a job. You're better of with Asquinns, finish school and get a proper job."

Martin reached over to an end table where a business sized envelope lay. He drew a document from inside and opened it.

"Is this good enough for you?' he asked Sihon and handed him the document.

Sihon took the single sheet of white paper, read it through. His eyes grew big as he looked from Martin to Audrey. Olvina, Phoebe, Kathleen, Cassis and Eunice smiled at him.

"This says Sihon Nigel Weistien- Asquinn. Does this mean you've adopted me?"

"We have," Audrey said.

Sihon said. He wiped a tear from the corner of one eye.

"Mom, Dad. I won't miss Cameron Estate or missing out on the millions Conrad wanted me to inherit. Olvina, Phoebe, Kathleen, Cassia and Eunice, are my family."

"I hope you consider the extended family as your own," Martha said.

"I do, Aunt Martha. I do," Sihon said. "I don't even feel a void now that Conrad and Lillian aren't here. Nothing. Only God's peace fills my heart."

MATTHEW 7:24-25-Therefore whosoever hearth these words of mine, and doeth them, I will liken him unto a wise man who built his house upon a rock: 25/And the rains descended and the floods came, and the winds blew, and beat upon the house; and it fell not: for it was founded upon a rock.

Contact Information

Grace Brooks can be contacted through her website:

WEBSITE:
HTTP://WWW.HEATHERRADFORD.WEEBLY.COM

GraceBrooks@lgbrooks1 on Twiiter.

My author page on Amazon.com:
amazon.com/author/amazon.com.christianautho

Other Books in The Asquinn Twins Series by Grace Brooks
1/The Asquinn Twins Come To Forest Lake
2/The Fork In The Trail.
3/No Greener Pastures.
4/Sihon.
5/Grardians of Forest Lake

GRACE BROOKS